NATIONAL
AUDUBON
SOCIETY®

FIRST
FIELD
GUIDE

TREES

NATIONAL AUDUBON SOCIETY®

FIRST FIELD GUIDE

TREES

Written by
Brian Cassie

Scholastic Inc.

New York   Toronto   London   Auckland   Sydney
Mexico City   New Delhi   Hong Kong

The National Audubon Society, established in 1905, has 550,000 members and more than 500 chapters nationwide. Its mission is to conserve and restore natural ecosystems, focusing on wildlife and plant life, and these guides are part of that mission. Celebrating the beauty and wonders of nature, Audubon looks toward its second century of educating people of all ages. For information about Audubon membership, contact:

National Audubon Society
700 Broadway
New York, NY 10003-9562
212-979-3000   800-274-4201
http://www.audubon.org

LIBRARY OF CONGRESS CATALOGING-IN-PUBLICATION DATA

Cassie, Brian, 1953–
  National Audubon Society first field guide. Trees / written by Brian Cassie.
    p.   cm.
  Includes bibliographical references (p.   ) and index.
  Summary: A visual guide to the natural science of trees as well as a field guide to the trees found in the United States and Canada.
  ISBN 0-590-05472-4 (hc) — ISBN 0-590-05490-2 (pb)
  1. Trees—United States—Identification—Juvenile literature.
2. Trees—Canada—Identification—Juvenile literature. 3. Trees—United States—Pictorial works—Juvenile literature. 4. Trees—Canada—Pictorial works—Juvenile literature [1. Trees.]
I. Title.
QK475.8.C37 1999
582.16'0973—dc21   98-21855

10 9 8 7 6 5 4 3 2 1   9/9   0/0   01   02   03

Printed in Hong Kong
First printing, April 1999

Contents

About this book

Osage Orange page 128

Whether you are looking at trees in your own yard, while taking a walk in the woods, or while on vacation in a wilderness park, this book will help you look at trees the way a naturalist does. The book has four parts:

PART 1: The world of trees tells you about the two main types of trees, explains how trees grow, describes the parts of a tree, and explores how trees affect the humans and the wildlife around them.

PART 2: How to look at trees gives you the information you need to begin identifying trees. You will learn where different types of trees grow, what shapes trees take, and how to identify trees by their leaves, flowers, fruits, and bark.

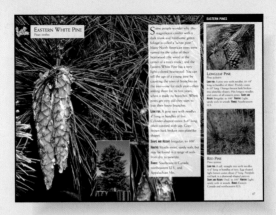

PART 3: The field guide includes detailed descriptions and dramatic photographs of 50 common North American trees. In addition, this section provides helpful shorter descriptions, with photographs, of nearly 100 other important species.

PART 4: The reference section at the back of the book includes an illustrated list of state trees; a helpful glossary of terms used by naturalists when they talk about trees; lists of useful books, Web sites, and organizations; a metric conversion chart; and an index of species covered in the field guide.

What is a naturalist?

A naturalist is a person who studies nature and shares that knowledge with others. A naturalist might study birds, toads, butterflies, trees, or a combination of things. People who become experts on trees or other kinds of plants are called botanists.

John Muir standing next to a Giant Sequoia (page 54)

The great outdoors

Some naturalists, like John Muir (1838–1914), spend years of their lives in the outdoors, looking, listening, and learning. Muir was interested in all of nature, but his specialty was trees. He worked tirelessly to save the great forests of Redwoods and other trees in California and to let the world know what treasures these majestic trees were. Muir wrote many books about his travels and discoveries. The greatest naturalists like to share their findings with other people.

YOU CAN BE A NATURALIST

Next time you are up a tree, you can start thinking like a naturalist. Just look closely and take notes about the tree's different parts. Use your own "natural" curiosity to ask questions and find out more about the trees in your area.

YOUR BOTANICAL TOOLS

When you go out to look at trees, take this field guide so you can identify the trees you see. You may also pack a camera and a notebook and pencils to draw or record your findings. If you have an unbreakable magnifying glass, you can use it to look closely at hard-to-see things, such as the tiny veins in a leaf. You might also take measuring tools: a ruler and a ball of twine (with scissors). To find out how big around a tree trunk is, wrap the twine around it, cut, and measure.

Rules for a naturalist

- When you go exploring, take a buddy with you. Tell a grown-up where you are going.

- Respect nature. Leave everything the way you found it. Don't trample plants, break branches, move fallen logs (insects and other animals, as well as plants, make their homes in them), or leave litter behind.

- In the wild, you can take a few sample leaves, flowers, fruits, or seeds without doing any harm. In a park or arboretum, take samples only if they are lying on the ground.

- Never taste a fruit or nut unless someone else (preferably an adult) has confirmed that it is safe to eat.

- Always ask permission before walking onto private property.

- Share your discoveries with others.

What is a tree?

Trees come in many different colors, sizes, and shapes. They can grow to a height of 20 feet or soar as high as a skyscraper. They can have purplish, heart-shaped leaves or bright green needles. They can grow in the shape of a cone or in the shape of an open umbrella. Even so, all trees, no matter what they look like, have some things in common.

Most trees are at least 20 feet tall when fully grown.

A tree is a large, woody plant that can live for many years— sometimes for hundreds or even thousands of years!

A tree has a single stem, or trunk, usually with no side branches for at least several feet above the ground.

Tree or shrub?

A shrub is a woody plant, like a tree. Most shrubs are shorter than trees and have several stems rising out of the ground instead of a single trunk. Shrubs usually don't have a crown of a definite shape.

This woody plant is a shrub.

The top of a tree is called its crown. A tree's crown often grows in a clear shape, depending on the type of tree it is.

These wildflowers are herbs.

Tree or herb?

A tree is a plant, just like the tulips and tomatoes in people's gardens and the wildflowers along the side of the road. But those green plants, called herbs, have fleshy stems, not woody ones like trees and shrubs. The stems dry up and often die in the winter.

11

The plant kingdom

This hickory has shaggy bark.

Scientists separate plants and animals into groups. Almost every living thing on earth is in either the plant kingdom or the animal kingdom. The plant kingdom is divided into groups called divisions. Each division is divided into classes, each class into orders, and each order into families. Every family is divided into genera (singular: genus), and each genus into species.

This pine has long needles.

WHAT'S ITS NAME?

What would you name a pine tree with needles up to 18 inches long? How about a hickory tree with shaggy bark? If you said "Longleaf Pine" and "Shagbark Hickory," you guessed the common names of these trees. The common name often gives you some useful information about the tree. For example, you can tell from their names where the Arizona Sycamore grows and that you have to be careful not to touch a Poison Sumac!

What is a species?

When we talk about a kind of animal or insect or tree, we are talking about a species. The Red-winged Blackbird is a species, and so is the White-tailed Deer. The Longleaf Pine is a species of tree. As with every species of animal and plant, all Longleaf Pine trees look pretty much alike and can produce offspring (new trees) that are the same as themselves.

Two species divided

The Longleaf Pine and the Shagbark Hickory are in the same kingdom and the same division, but they part company at the class level. They're divided there because of an important difference in the way they bear their seeds.

Kingdom: Plantae
Division: Spermatophta
Class: Angiospermae
Order: Juglandales
Family: Juglandaceae
Genus: *Carya*
Species: *ovata*
(Shagbark Hickory)

Kingdom: Plantae
Division: Spermatophta
Class: Gymnospermae
Order: Coniferales
Family: Pinaceae
Genus: *Pinus*
Species: *palustris*
(Longleaf Pine)

How do you think the Paper Birch (page 74) got its name?

Species names

Every species of tree has a common name and a scientific name. The scientific name is known and used by botanists all over the world. Longleaf Pine's scientific name is *Pinus palustris*, Shagbark Hickory's is *Carya ovata*, and the Paper Birch's is *Betula papyrifera*. The first word in the scientific name indicates the genus, or group, to which the tree belongs. The Longleaf Pine (*Pinus palustris*) and the Lodgepole Pine (*Pinus contorta*) both belong to the genus *Pinus*. All trees in the genus *Pinus* are pines.

Two classes of trees

Can you see the two main types of trees?

If you take a walk in the woods, you will probably notice that there are two main kinds of trees that look very different from each other. One kind is the nonflowering, needleleaf trees, most of which have leaves shaped like needles that stay on the tree all year. The other kind is the flowering, broadleaf trees, which have wide, flat leaves that usually fall off the tree in autumn.

Needlelike leaves

Scalelike leaves

Needleleaf trees

The needleleaf trees do not produce flowers. Their seeds do not grow inside a fruit or nut. Their leaves mainly look like green needles, although some species have leaves that look like scales. Most needleleaf trees are evergreens, which means they don't lose their leaves in winter.

CONIFERS

Most of the world's needleleaf trees are conifers, trees that produce cones. The seed of a conifer does not grow inside a protective container like a fruit or nut. The ripening seeds of conifers are tucked between the scales of the cone and fall out when they are ready. Pines, spruces, and firs are all conifers.

Douglas Fir cones page 52

Flowering Dogwood page 134

Broadleaf trees

The broadleaf trees are flowering trees. The seeds of flowering trees are hidden inside a container that may be fleshy, like the crisp, juicy part of an apple, or dry, like the shell of a nut. The container of the seed is called a fruit no matter what it looks like. Most broadleaf trees are deciduous, which means the leaves fall off in autumn. Some species of broadleaf trees, like rhododendrons, have tough, leathery leaves that stay on the tree year-round.

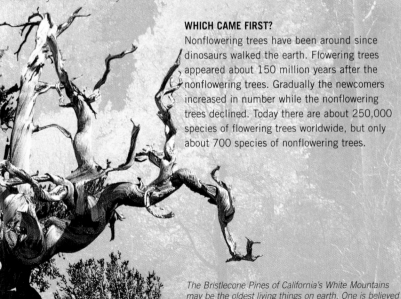

WHICH CAME FIRST?

Nonflowering trees have been around since dinosaurs walked the earth. Flowering trees appeared about 150 million years after the nonflowering trees. Gradually the newcomers increased in number while the nonflowering trees declined. Today there are about 250,000 species of flowering trees worldwide, but only about 700 species of nonflowering trees.

The Bristlecone Pines of California's White Mountains may be the oldest living things on earth. One is believed to be almost 5,000 years old!

15

Anatomy of a tree

Just as all the parts of your body work together to help you grow and stay healthy, a tree has parts that help it grow and stay healthy, too. The main parts of a tree are its roots, shoot system (the trunk and branches), and leaves.

Putting down roots

A tree's roots have two important jobs: They anchor the tree in the ground, and they take up water and minerals from the soil to help feed the tree. The roots spread out in all directions, but most remain in the top four feet of soil, where most of the water and minerals are.

The ring thing

Every year a tree's trunk grows wider. Each year's growth appears as a ring. You can count the rings in a sawed-off tree trunk to see how old the tree was.

bark

The wood in the center of a tree trunk is called the heartwood. It is dead wood and is usually dark.

The lighter wood outside the heartwood is called the sapwood. The tree's sap (water and nutrients) flows up and down in the sapwood.

The food-making leaves

Trees make their own food inside the leaves. This way of making food is called photosynthesis. The ingredients are sunlight, water, minerals from the soil, and carbon dioxide, a gas in the air that animals give off when breathing out. The leaves give off oxygen, the gas in the air that animals breathe in.

Every leaf has tiny holes called stomata. Carbon dioxide from the air enters a leaf through the stomata. Oxygen exits the leaf through the stomata. Some of the oxygen is used by the tree, but most of it is released into the air.

The pipelines

A tree's main stem (the trunk) supports the branches, and the branches support the leaves. The trunk and branches also serve as pipelines, carrying water, nutrients, and minerals from the roots to the leaves. They also carry food made by the leaves back to the rest of the tree to be used or stored.

Taking a stand for trees

For hundreds of years people have been cutting down the trees of North America. Trees are cut so that land can be cleared for building and farming, as well as for their wood. The wood is used for many things, including houses, ships, furniture, and railroads. Now people are fighting to save the North American forests.

Why are living trees so important?

There are lots of reasons. Trees filter pollution out of water and air. They help prevent flooding and soil erosion. They give us shade and block the wind. They provide homes and food for mammals, birds, and insects. They give off the oxygen that all animals breathe. A healthy tree can supply one person with all the oxygen he or she needs in a day.

Get out there and plant some trees!

How much can one person do?

It's hard to imagine what western North America would look like today if John Muir hadn't been so captivated by its beauty. He was a conservation pioneer, helping to save millions of acres of forests and to convince the U.S. government to set aside certain lands, including Yosemite Valley, as national parks. Andy Lipkis was a teenager in 1973 when he started a group in Los Angeles called TreePeople, whose mission was—and still is—to plant trees in cities and forests to improve the environment.

Old-growth forest, Washington

Old-growth forests

Forests that have been growing undisturbed for many years are called old-growth forests. These forests have huge trees that are hundreds of years old. Standing dead trees, called snags, provide homes for animals. New trees sprout on rotting logs, which supply the saplings with nutrients and moisture.

LOGGING OLD-GROWTH FORESTS

Most of North America's old-growth forests have been destroyed in the last 300 years. Some of the few remaining forests are in danger of being cut down by logging companies. Although these companies plant new trees, it takes hundreds of years for an old-growth forest to form.

19

White-tailed Deer gnawing on oak branch

Trees and animals

Trees and animals relate to one another in many ways. Some of these are easy to see in the wild—and can even help us to identify trees. Birds, mammals, and insects live in trees and feed on their fruit, leaves, and flowers. What do trees get out of the relationship? They get their flowers fertilized and their seeds scattered around, so that new trees can grow.

Mammals

High above the ground in the great western forests of Douglas Fir trees lives a tiny mammal, the Red Tree Vole. This little rodent lives its entire life in the tree's branches. Most mammals are not so closely tied to one species of tree, but trees are very important to many mammals, small and large.

Red Squirrel with stash of pinecones. Some of the cones will drop their seeds and sprout new trees.

American Beaver chewing willow twigs

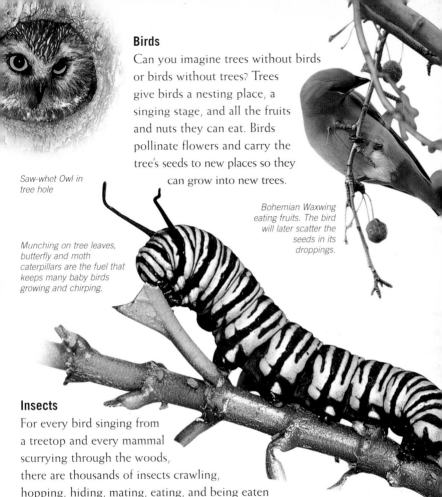

Birds

Can you imagine trees without birds or birds without trees? Trees give birds a nesting place, a singing stage, and all the fruits and nuts they can eat. Birds pollinate flowers and carry the tree's seeds to new places so they can grow into new trees.

Saw-whet Owl in tree hole

Bohemian Waxwing eating fruits. The bird will later scatter the seeds in its droppings.

Munching on tree leaves, butterfly and moth caterpillars are the fuel that keeps many baby birds growing and chirping.

Insects

For every bird singing from a treetop and every mammal scurrying through the woods, there are thousands of insects crawling, hopping, hiding, mating, eating, and being eaten in the trees of North American forests, parks, and backyards.

Many insects, such as the Spruce Budworm and the Gypsy Moth, are terribly destructive to our trees, but on the whole, insects add much more than they take away.

Bees buzz from blossom to blossom on fruit trees, collecting nectar and fertilizing flowers so that fruits will form.

21

How forests grow

In many parts of North America, if a field is left alone and not used for farming or other things, trees will begin to grow in it. Over many years' time, a forest will form.

Field to forest

The first trees to grow in an open field are called pioneers. They are trees that like sunshine, don't live very long, and grow fast. Following the pioneers are trees that can grow in shade, like oaks and maples. They sprout and grow in the shade of the pioneers. When they grow larger, they shade out the pioneers, and the pioneers die off.

In eastern North America, Eastern Red Cedars (pictured; page 59) and Gray Birches are often the pioneers in a field.

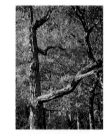

Oaks (pictured) and maples follow the pioneers in the East, often forming a shady grove.

In western North America, Quaking Aspens (page 66) are often the first trees to grow in a clearing.

Forest fires

Parts of the western United States are regularly swept by wildfires. Although you might think these fires are all bad, they aren't. Some plants and trees can't grow without fire. Many conifers don't release the seeds from their cones until there is a fire. The fire's heat makes the cones open up, and then the seeds fall out. The ash from a fire makes the soil very nutritious, so that a new forest can begin to grow.

Fireweed is one of the first plants to grow after a fire. Here it grows with Lodgepole Pine saplings (page 49).

Lodgepole Pine cones are tightly closed until the heat of a fire opens them up, making the seeds fall out.

Needleleaf trees such as Engelmann Spruce (page 51) commonly follow pioneer trees in the West.

Where do trees grow?

Trees grow almost everywhere in North America except the highest mountaintops and the far northern tundra. But while trees can be found almost any place you look, most species of trees can grow only in certain conditions, and many species grow only in certain places. Some of the things that determine where a tree can grow include climate, altitude, soil type, sunlight, and rainfall.

Coastlines

Some trees thrive in the loose, sandy soil and salty air of coastal areas. Along the coast of northern Washington and southern British Columbia, the mild winters and plentiful moisture support a rain forest of pines, Douglas Fir, Sitka Spruce, and Western Red Cedar. Pines, including Longleaf and Loblolly, dominate on the sandy coastal plains of the East, along with a variety of oaks and hickories.

Redwoods (page 55) grow on the western slopes of the Coast Ranges in western North America. In summer, when currents of warm air from the Pacific Ocean meet cooler air over the land, the trees are bathed in fog. The fog drips onto the ground, where it is taken up by the trees' roots.

Needleleaf trees, pictured here along the Strait of Juan de Fuca, Washington, thrive along coastlines.

Habitat and range

Knowing where a tree species grows can help you identify the trees that you see. A tree's range is the geographical area where it can be found. The range is always a place, like Alaska or eastern Canada. A tree's habitat is a certain type of place where the living conditions (such as temperature, amount of water, and type of soil) suit the tree's needs. The range of the Red Maple, for example, is eastern North America, but you won't see one unless you look in its habitat—wet or swampy areas.

Bald Cypresses (page 56) grow in freshwater swamps in the southeastern United States. Flared trunks and knobby growths called knees help the trees absorb extra oxygen.

Wetlands

Some trees grow in wetlands, which are areas with standing water on the ground. Wetlands of North America include the banks of streams, rivers, lakes, and ponds, as well as swamps and marshes. Some swamps and marshes near the coast are tidal, which means they are flooded with salt water whenever the tide comes in. Red Mangroves, Black Mangroves, Bald Cypresses, Water Tupelos, Red Maples, and Silver Maples all grow in swamps.

Eastern Cottonwoods (page 67), shown here on the Missouri River, grow on riverbanks, where the soil is moist and nutritious. Black Cottonwood, Mountain Alder, and Black Willow are other waterside species.

The needlelike leaves of the Joshua Tree (page 62) do not dry up in the desert heat.

HOT AND DRY

Desert trees have many tricks for surviving in their dry habitat. To avoid losing water through its leaves, the Blue Paloverde sheds them soon after they come out in spring. The job of making food is done by its blue-green branches and twigs. The Screwbean Mesquite sends its roots down 60 feet or more to find groundwater. The Mohave Yucca stores water in its fleshy, expandable trunk.

Open areas

While many trees grow in forests, some trees like wide-open areas with lots of sunshine and dry soil. Canyon and Interior Live Oaks grow in California's foothill grasslands. European Buckthorn and Bur Oak grow in the grasslands of the Midwest.

Interior Live Oak in Sierra Nevada foothills

Mountains

Trees that grow in mountains must be able to survive in severe cold, heavy snow, and high winds. Most mountains are wet on one side and dry on the other, so different trees grow on either side. The highest areas of mountains are above the treeline, where no trees grow. Among the trees that grow well on mountains are pines, spruces, and firs.

Needleleaf trees, such as these in San Bernardino National Forest, California, clothe many high mountain slopes.

Tree shapes

Have you ever seen a tree shaped like a triangle, pointed at the top and flared at the bottom? It was probably a member of the pine family. When you are identifying trees, sometimes a tree's overall shape can give you an important clue. Each species of tree has its own growth pattern, which means it tends to grow in a particular shape. However, trees don't always follow the pattern exactly, and most trees change their shape as they get older. But if you look at the shape along with other clues, such as bark pattern and leaf type, you will learn to identify many of the trees you see.

Triangular trees, like the White Spruce (page 50), are pointed at the top and flared at the bottom.

Wide-spreading trees, like the Live Oak (page 83), are wider than they are tall.

Basic shapes

These pictures show some basic tree shapes. Sometimes the shape is easier to see when the leaves have fallen. The left side of each picture shows the tree in summer or fall and the right side shows it in winter.

Oval trees, like the Sugar Maple (page 118), can be just a little higher than wide or can form a very tall, narrow oval.

The branches of fan-shaped and vase-shaped trees, like the American Elm (page 88), rise upward and then spread wide in a graceful curve.

The branches of drooping trees like the Weeping Willow hang down toward the ground.

LOST IN THE CROWD

When a tree grows by itself in a place with lots of space and sunshine, like in a field or park, it will grow in the special shape of its species. But if it is crowded with other trees, or grows in a shady spot between buildings, its shape will be different. Its branches will reach up toward the sun, and lower branches that never get any sun will drop off. Tree shape works best as a clue for trees that stand alone.

How to tell trees by their leaves

Most people identify trees by looking at the leaves. The first thing you will notice about a tree's leaves is whether they are broad leaves or needle leaves. Once you know that, there are different things to look at for each type.

When you look at a wooded hillside in summer, what do you see? Just a lot of green! But look at the same hill in fall, and you can pick out dark green pines, bright yellow aspens, and scarlet-red maples.

Needles

The needleleaf trees have needle-shaped leaves or scalelike leaves. Most needleleaf trees are evergreens, keeping their needles through the winter. Many needle leaves have a thick, waxy skin that keeps them from losing too much water. Pines, larches, spruces, hemlocks, and firs all have needle leaves. Pines are easy to tell from the others because they bear their leaves in bundles of two to five needles. Cedars and junipers are evergreens with scalelike leaves.

The Eastern White Pine (page 46) is the only pine east of the Rockies that has five needles in a bundle.

Among the pines, the odd one is the Singleleaf Pinyon. Its name tells you how it differs.

Spruce needles are shorter than pine needles, grow singly (not in bundles), and are usually stiff and sharp-pointed.

Spruces grow stems of bright green new needles in spring.

Leaves of larches, including the Tamarack, grow in tufts and turn yellow before falling off in winter.

Hemlock needles are flat and flexible and have a short stalk that attaches to a round, woody "cushion."

Douglas Fir (page 52) needles are flat and soft, and each needle grows on a short, twisted stalk.

Bald Cypress (page 56) needles are mostly flat and soft and, like larch needles, they fall off in winter.

The Redwood (page 55) has two kinds of leaves: flat, stiff, sharp needles, and short scalelike leaves.

Trees with scalelike leaves include the Giant Sequoia, cypresses, and cedars.

Leaves of broadleaf trees

The flowering trees have broad leaves, which are usually flat and wide. They include maples, oaks, poplars, willows, and hundreds of others. Their leaves vary in shape and size and in the position they take on the twig. They have many different kinds of margins, or edges: toothed or untoothed, wavy, curled under, or prickly. They can be lobed (divided into "fingers"). They can be simple (one leaf on each stalk) or compound (divided into many separate leaflets on each stalk). And, of course, they come in many different shades of green and often have one shade on top and another underneath.

LEAF ARRANGEMENTS

paired, compound

unpaired

whorled

Sometimes the way the leaves are arranged on the twig can give you a clue about what type of tree it is. Paired leaves (or leaflets, in compound leaves) grow next to each other, one on each side of the stalk. Unpaired leaves alternate on the stalk. Whorled leaves grow in a circle.

LOBED, TOOTHED, OR UNTOOTHED?

Lobed leaves have deep indentations in their edges. They may be shaped like a star, a mitten, or a hand.

The edges of toothed leaves are jagged, like the blade of a saw.

The edges of untoothed leaves are smooth.

32

LEAF SHAPES

Eastern Redbud (page 110) has unpaired, simple, untoothed, heart-shaped leaves with long stalks.

Birch leaves are unpaired, simple, triangular, and toothed. Their long, pointed tips help drain off rainwater.

Some simple leaves, like those of willow trees, are long and thin.

Northern Red Oak (page 84) leaves are unpaired, simple, and lobed.

White Oak (page 82) leaves have rounded lobes.

Maple leaves are lobed and toothed and have a long red or green stalk. This is a Sugar Maple (page 118) leaf.

Oak leaves have one central vein (like a feather), but maple veins, as shown here, fan outward like a hand.

Sweetgum (page 96) leaves are lobed and look like maple leaves but are shaped more like stars than like hands.

The leaves of buckeyes are compound and whorled, with the leaflets spreading out from a central point.

Sumac leaves are compound, with paired leaflets lined up along both sides of the stalk like the barbs of a feather.

Some broadleaf trees, like this Southern Magnolia (page 92) are evergreen. Their leaves are usually leathery, shiny, and untoothed.

33

Flowers

A flowering plant, whether it is a massive sycamore or a humble dandelion, has flowers. Some tree flowers are very small and hardly noticeable; others completely cover the tree at flowering time. Each tree species has a particular time of year that suits it best for flowering.

Pollen blown by the wind

Why do trees have flowers?

Flowers contain the parts of plants that make the seeds so that new plants can grow. In order for this process to begin, the flower must be pollinated. This means that the flower's pollen must be carried to another flower or to another part of the same flower. Once a flower has been pollinated, the fruit and seeds can develop. Wind, insects, and birds help to move pollen from one flower to another.

Tulip Tree flower page 93

American Elm flowers page 88

Early spring

Trees that burst into bloom in early spring usually have outstanding numbers of flowers. But the flowers tend to be quite small and sometimes just look like a faint haze of color on the branches. Willows, elms, poplars, redbuds, ashes, and maples all flower very early, usually before their leaves appear. Take a close look at those trees that start to change color early in spring. You'll probably see some great little flowers.

Norway Maple flowers page 122

Sassafras flowers page 94

American Sycamore
flowers page 98

Spring

Some of the most familiar and
widespread trees, such as oaks, walnuts,
sycamores, beeches, Tulip Trees,
Sassafras, and Sweetgum, get their
flowers in spring just as their leaves are
unfolding. These numerous but mostly
small flowers often get lost in the new
greenery. If you take the time to
examine these trees or look on the
ground under them, you'll find all kinds
and colors of interesting flowers.

Southern Catalpa flowers page 140

Crabapple flowers

Late spring to early summer

Trees that blossom in late spring or early summer have blooms that are
usually very showy—large or colorful or abundant or all three. Cherries
and other fruit trees, magnolias, hawthorns, locusts, buckeyes, and catalpas
all fit into this group. When a tree is fully leafed out, it has to have showy
flowers so that the insects that pollinate them can find them easily.

Better late than never

Long after all the other trees in the woods
have flowered and set their fruit, even after
a lot of the fruits and nuts have fallen from
or been eaten from these trees, one tree just
gets around to blooming. In the fall,
look for the spidery, yellow flowers
of the Witch Hazel. Since
the Witch Hazel is a
spreading, low-growing
tree, most of its flowers are
down near eye level, where
they are easy to see.

Witch Hazel flowers page 97

Fruits, nuts, and cones

Fruits, nuts, and cones are the parts of a tree that contain its seeds. They are often very showy, staying on trees for long periods and then littering the ground when they fall off. Many fruits can help us tell families and species of trees apart.

Nuts

Many trees grow nuts. Some nuts are large; others are small. They come in a variety of shapes. American Chestnuts, Horse Chestnuts, chinkapins, and buckeyes all have large, smooth, shiny nuts encased in prickly husks. Nuts of hickories and walnuts are also large, but their husks are relatively smooth and not easily confused with chestnuts and buckeyes. Take special care telling edible American Chestnuts and chinkapins from poisonous Horse Chestnuts and buckeyes—never eat any of these nuts unless you are positive of their identification.

*American Chestnuts
page 81*

ACORNS

Acorns, which grow on oak trees, are the most well-known nuts on North American trees. All oaks produce acorns, but not all acorns look alike. Some are long and skinny, others are short and plump, and still others have fringed cups. Examining acorns closely can often help you tell one oak tree from another.

White Oak acorn page 82   *Northern Red Oak acorns page 84*

Fleshy fruits

The trees of the rose family give us our finest tree fruits. Apples, cherries, pears, peaches, and plums are all members of the rose family. Their fruits are the main reason this family of trees is so widely planted around North America. Fleshy fruits of other trees outside the rose family, such as Persimmon and Pawpaw, make identification of these trees easy when they are in fruit.

Common Apple page 100

Winged fruits

Winged fruits, or keys, grow in clusters on maples and ashes. When the keys ripen, they break off the tree and twirl down to the ground like little helicopters. The wings help carry the seeds away from the parent tree, where they have a better chance to grow into trees themselves. Maple keys grow in pairs, while those of ashes grow singly. The angle between pairs of maple keys is different on different kinds of maples and helps us tell one species from another.

Red Maple keys page 119

White Ash keys page 142

Tamarack cones page 53

Cones

Conifers, such as firs, pines, and spruces, grow tough, woody cones to hold and protect their seeds. The cones of some trees hang down, while others stand upright on the branches. Some cones are as big as a grapefruit, while others are just a little bigger than a pea.

Douglas Fir cones page 52

Eastern Redbud pods page 110

Pods

Trees of the pea family grow their seeds in pods. If you find a tree that is covered with fruits that look like pea pods or bean pods, it belongs to the pea family. Look at the different colors, shapes, and sizes of the pods. They can be a big help in telling one pea-family tree from another.

40

Sumacs and dogwoods

Sumac fruits

The fruits of sumacs and dogwoods, which look like red berries (but are not edible), stay on the trees into the winter. Whether you live in Texas or Maine or somewhere in-between, you can easily recognize sumacs by their big clusters of small, red, hairy fruits. Long after their flowers have faded, Pacific and Flowering dogwoods are easy to spot by their tiny, red, football-shaped fruits.

Sycamores and Sweetgum

All fruits and nuts beautify the trees they grow on, but some of the fruits look more like mere decorations than fruits. Sycamores and Sweetgum have round, ball-like fruits that make them easy to identify. When the fruits fall to the ground, they are often collected for wreaths and other ornaments.

Sweetgum fruit page 96

How do seeds travel?

Seeds travel in many different ways. Some have wings or parachutes and are blown by the wind. Some ride inside a fruit that can be eaten by an animal. Some, such as coconuts, float away on water.

Witch Hazel (page 97) seeds are scattered when they burst out of the fruits.

Bark

A tree's bark is there to protect the tree from excessive heat or cold, insect damage, pollution, lawn mowers banging up against it, and the other things trees have to put up with while they are standing in one spot. A tree cannot survive without its bark.

What to look for

Many species of trees have gray to brown bark, but some have red, orange, white, or multicolored bark. Lots of trees have rough bark that is broken into ridges and plates. Others have shreddy, spiny, smooth, peeling, or flaky barks. The combination of bark color and texture is often enough to identify a tree even if there are no leaves or flowers or fruits present.

ELASTIC BARK

On all trees, bark is stretched as the tree grows. On some trees, such as birches and American Beeches, the bark is elastic and stretches without breaking. That's why these trees have such smooth bark. On other trees, such as oaks, the outer layers of bark break when they are stretched too far. This makes the bark rough and sculptured.

American Beech bark page 80

CHANGING WITH AGE

Look at a young Black Cherry tree (shown at left, top). Notice that the bark is dark brown, smooth, and marked with white horizontal lines . Now look at a mature Black Cherry (left, bottom). See how the bark has turned blackish (that's where the tree's name comes from) and has broken into small, squarish plates. As a tree grows, its bark will very likely change color and texture. In the field guide section of this book, most of the bark descriptions are for full-grown trees.

Black Cherry bark page 103

SHREDDING, FLAKING, AND PEELING BARK

Some trees always seem to be losing pieces of their bark in strips and flakes. Birch bark peels around the trunk, cedar and eucalyptus bark peels lengthwise, and sycamores, madrones, and Ponderosa Pines litter the ground beneath their trunks with good-sized flakes of bark. The famous bark of the Shagbark Hickory looks as though it will fall off at any time, but actually it is firmly attached to the trunk.

THE THICKEST BARK

Redwoods and Giant Sequoias have the thickest bark of any trees. Redwood bark can be up to one foot thick and deeply fissured, while Giant Sequoias can have bark twice as thick— two feet! Because the bark of these monstrous trees has almost no sap, it makes the trees virtually fireproof. The great thickness of the bark also keeps insects at bay.

Giant Sequoia bark page 54

BRIGHTLY COLORED BARK

The peeling, flaking nature of Pacific Madrone and sycamore bark, along with the interesting color combinations that result when different layers of bark are exposed as the outer bark peels away, make these trees popular with landowners. Why have plain gray bark when you can have lots of color? For this reason, the Red Osier Dogwood, with its brilliant red bark, is commonly planted in gardens and yards.

Pacific Madrone bark page 138

Using the field guide

This section features 50 common North American trees and includes brief descriptions of 95 more. Color photographs and details about each tree help you identify it. The trees on the facing page either are related to the main species or share some characteristics, such as appearance and habitat.

Quaking Aspen page 66

ICONS

These icons appear on each left-hand page in the field guide. They help you find a featured tree in the guide by the kind of leaves it has.

Needleleaf Trees

Broadleaf Trees: Lobed leaves

Palms & Yuccas

Broadleaf Trees: Compound leaves

Broadleaf Trees: Simple-shaped leaves

Flowering Dogwood page 134

LEAF ICON
This icon helps you find a featured tree by the kind of leaves it has.

BOX HEADING
The box heading alerts you to other trees covered in the box that are similar in some way to the main tree on the page.

NAME
The common and scientific names appear here.

EASTERN PINES

EASTERN WHITE PINE
Pinus strobus

Some people wonder why this magnificent conifer with a dark trunk and handsome green foliage is called a "white pine." Many North American trees were named for the color of their heartwood (the wood at the center of a tree's trunk), and the Eastern White Pine has a very light-colored heartwood. You can tell the age of a young pine by counting the rows of branches on the tree—one for each year—then adding three for its first years, when it made no branches. When pines get very old they start to lose their lower branches.

LOOK FOR: A pine tree with needles 4" long in bundles of five. Cylinder-shaped cones 5–6" long, often covered with sap. Gray-brown bark broken into platelike shapes.

SHAPE AND HEIGHT: Irregular, to 100'.

HABITAT: Mostly moist, sandy soils, but may be found in a range of soils from dry to swampy.

RANGE: Southeastern Canada, northeastern U.S., and Appalachian Mts.

LONGLEAF PINE
Pinus palustris
LOOK FOR: A pine tree with needles 10–18" long in bundles of three. Prickly cones 6–10" long. Orange-brown bark broken into platelike shapes. Has longest needles and cones of all eastern pines. **SHAPE AND HEIGHT:** Irregular, to 100'. **HABITAT:** Light, sandy soils in woods. **RANGE:** Southeastern U.S.

RED PINE
Pinus resinosa
LOOK FOR: A tall, straight tree with needles 4–6" long in bundles of two. Egg-shaped, light brown cones about 2" long. Purplish-red bark in a diamond-shaped pattern. **SHAPE AND HEIGHT:** Oval, to 100'. **RANGE:** Light, sandy soils in woods. **RANGE:** Eastern Canada and northeastern U.S.

47

IDENTIFICATION CAPSULE
The identification capsule gives you the details you need to identify a tree: shape, height, color and arrangement of leaves and flowers, and descriptions of its bark, fruits, nuts, and more.

HABITAT AND RANGE
The range and habitat listings tell you at a glance whether or not a tree is likely to be seen in your area.

CAUTION
Some pages have caution labels, following the range listings, to alert you to plants that are prickly, poisonous to eat, or cause reactions such as rashes.

EASTERN WHITE PINE
Pinus strobus

Some people wonder why this magnificent conifer with a dark trunk and handsome green foliage is called a "white pine." Many North American trees were named for the color of their heartwood (the wood at the center of a tree's trunk), and the Eastern White Pine has a very light-colored heartwood. You can tell the age of a young pine by counting the rows of branches on the tree—one for each year—then adding three for its first years, when it made no branches. When pines get very old they start to lose their lower branches.

Look for: A pine tree with needles 4" long in bundles of five. Cylinder-shaped cones 5–6" long, often covered with sap. Gray-brown bark broken into platelike shapes.

Shape and Height: Irregular; to 100'.

Habitat: Mostly moist, sandy soils, but may be found in a range of soils from dry to swampy.

Range: Southeastern Canada, northeastern U.S., and Appalachian Mts.

LONGLEAF PINE
Pinus palustris

Look for: A pine tree with needles 10–18" long in bundles of three. Prickly cones 6–10" long. Orange-brown bark broken into platelike shapes. Has longest needles and cones of all eastern pines. **Shape and Height:** Irregular; to 100'. **Habitat:** Light, sandy soils in woods. **Range:** Southeastern U.S.

RED PINE
Pinus resinosa

Look for: A tall, straight tree with needles 4–6" long in bundles of two. Egg-shaped, light brown cones about 2" long. Purplish-red bark in a diamond-shaped pattern. **Shape and Height:** Oval; to 100'. **Habitat:** Light, sandy soils in woods. **Range:** Eastern Canada and northeastern U.S.

PONDEROSA PINE
Pinus ponderosa

The American West is home to a great number of conifers—this is their region above all others. Ponderosa Pine may be the most widespread conifer and is probably the most abundant western tree of any kind. Ponderosas don't like to crowd each other, so their aromatic forests are usually quite sunny and easy to hike through. Look at the base of these trees to find fallen bark pieces in jigsaw-puzzle shapes.

Look for: Yellow-green needles up to 10" long in bundles of two or three. Oval cones 3–6" long. Yellowish-red bark broken into large, smooth plates.

Shape and Height: Triangular; to 150'.

Habitat: Sandy soils in mountains.

Range: British Columbia and western U.S.

CONE

LODGEPOLE PINE
Pinus contorta

Look for: A fairly short, straight pine with needles 1–2" long in bundles of two. Prickly cones 1–2" long. Bark yellowish. Grows in groves. Unique because it is the only conifer native to both Alaska and Mexico. **Shape and Height:** Oval; to 80'. **Habitat:** High mountains. **Range:** Alaska, western Canada, and western U.S. into Mexico.

PINYON
Pinus edulis

Look for: A short, scrubby pine with needles 1–2" long in bundles of two. 2"-long cones produce two ½"-long, edible pine nuts per scale. Bark grayish-brown. **Shape and Height:** Oval; to 40'. **Habitat:** Dry, rocky soils in mountains. **Range:** Southwestern U.S., including Colorado.

49

WHITE SPRUCE
Picea glauca

Look at a White Spruce and you'll see a tree designed to shed snow. Its steeply angled sides keep snow from snapping its branches. The White Spruce is found throughout the North Woods of Canada, where winter snows are plentiful. Spruce Grouse, Boreal Chickadees, and Evening Grosbeaks keep year-round company with this northern conifer.

Look for: A straight, pointed tree. Blue-green needles about ½" long, 4-sided, and stiff (but not sharp). Its egg-shaped brown cones are about 2" long, have smooth-edged scales, and cluster together at the top of the tree.

Shape and Height: Triangular; to 75'.

Habitat: Moist soils along streams and lakes.

Range: Alaska, most of Canada, and northern U.S.

ENGELMANN SPRUCE
Picea engelmannii

Look for: A tall, pointed conifer growing in dense forests. Needles 1" long, 4-sided, and often sharp. Yellow-brown to reddish-brown cones ½–2" long, with ragged-edged scales. Often grows with Subalpine Fir in dark forests. **Shape and Height:** Triangular; to 125'. **Habitat:** Dense forests on moist mountain slopes. **Range:** Rocky Mts. in Canada and U.S.

BLUE SPRUCE
Picea pungens

Look for: Light gray-blue, sharp, stiff needles. Cones 2½–4" long. Foliage bluer in cultivated trees than in the wild. Gray or brown bark more furrowed than Engelmann Spruce. **Shape and Height:** Triangular; to 100'. **Habitat:** Moist soils along mountain streams and in urban areas. **Range:** Rocky Mts. in U.S.; widely planted throughout continent.

CONES

DOUGLAS FIR
Pseuodotsuga menziesii

The Douglas Fir is one of the three monster trees of the West (along with the Giant Sequoia and the Redwood). Walk in a Douglas Fir forest at noon on a sunny day and you'll be amazed at how the treetops block the sunlight—these trees love to grow close together. Douglas Firs can live to be 1,000 years old. Their branches provide food and shelter for Spotted Owls, Red Tree Voles, and other creatures.

LOOK FOR: Soft, blunt needles 1–1½" long, white-striped beneath. Egg-shaped, 2"-long cones with thin scales, distributed throughout tree. Dark, thick bark with deep vertical ridges.

SHAPE AND HEIGHT: Triangular; to 250'.

HABITAT: Moist soils from sea level to mountains.

RANGE: Southwestern Canada and western U.S.

EASTERN HEMLOCK
Tsuga canadensis

LOOK FOR: A handsome evergreen with soft foliage. Dark green needles ½" long, flattened, with rounded tips and 2 white lines beneath. Light brown, rounded cones ½–¾" long. Top of tree often bent over. Hemlocks are favorite nesting sites for several northern songbirds. **SHAPE AND HEIGHT:** Triangular; to 75'. **HABITAT:** Moist, cool soils, especially in shadowy ravines. **RANGE:** Eastern Canada, northeastern U.S., and Appalachian Mts.

TAMARACK
Larix laricina

LOOK FOR: An open-branched conifer. Blue-green needles ¾–1¼" long in bunches along twigs; turn yellow and fall off in autumn. Small, light brown cones similar to hemlock's. **SHAPE AND HEIGHT:** Triangular; to 80'. **HABITAT:** Wet soils, especially in bogs and swamps; to the treeline in northern tundra. **RANGE:** Alaska, Canada, Great Lakes region, and northeastern U.S.

53

GIANT SEQUOIA
Sequioadendron giganteum

CONES

Known locally as the Big Tree, the Giant Sequoia is the largest tree in the world, although not as tall as the more slender Redwood. There is no confusing this tree with the Redwood, as the two species grow in completely different regions. The best place to see the Big Tree is at Sequoia National Park's Giant Forest. Trees such as "General Sherman" and "General Grant" are thousands of years old and over 265 feet tall, with 36- to 40-foot-wide bases and lower branches over 100 feet long. Sequoia roots are not deep, but one tree's roots may spread out over three acres.

Look for: An enormous tree. Its blue-green, pointed leaves and reddish-brown cones are so high up that they are hard to see without binoculars. Has shreddy bark up to 24" thick.

Shape and Height: Tall, narrow oval; to 300'.

Habitat: Rocky, sandy soils on western side of mountains.

Range: Western Sierra Nevada in California.

Redwood
Sequoia sempervirens

Look for: The world's tallest tree and main tree of northern California's big coastal valley forests. Bark about 12" thick. Disease-proof. Roots are 100' deep, but these enormously tall and heavy trees die from toppling in high winds. **Shape and Height:** Tall, narrow oval; to 350' (record 368' in Redwood National Park). **Habitat:** Moist soils in foggy valleys. **Range:** California's Coast Ranges and southwestern corner of Oregon.

BALD CYPRESS
Taxodium distichum

In swamps of the Southeast—where Spanish Moss hangs on tree branches and herons lurk in the shallows, hunting frogs and sunfish—the great Bald Cypresses spread their trunks out into the murky waters. To best appreciate the Bald Cypress in its watery domain, canoe through a swamp. Watch out for alligators!

Look for: A swampland tree with a trunk that is wider at its base. Pale green needles and twigs fall in autumn. Round cones about 1" long. Branches often draped with Spanish Moss. Cone-shaped stumps called "knees" around the base help to provide air for the tree.

Shape and Height: Oval; to 125'.

Habitat: Swamps and other wet areas.

Range: Atlantic and Gulf coasts from Chesapeake Bay to Texas.

PACIFIC YEW
Taxus brevifolia

Look for: A tree with very dark foliage. Needles ½–1" long, dark green above and yellow-green below on green twigs. Seeds have brilliant red, fruitlike covering; open at one end showing dark seed inside. **Shape and Height:** Oval; to 40'. **Habitat:** Understory of moist forests. **Range:** Pacific Coast from southeastern Alaska to central California; parts of British Columbia and Idaho. **Caution:** Needles and seeds poisonous.

GINKGO
Ginkgo biloba

Look for: A unique tree with leaves that are shaped like fans, each with a notch in the center. Leaves turn yellow in autumn. Yellow-orange, plumlike seeds on female trees have disagreeable odor as they ripen. Male trees more widely planted than females. An ancient tree that dates back to the days of the dinosaurs. Native to Far East. **Shape and Height:** Oval; to 100'. **Habitat:** Planted in urban areas along streets and in parks. **Range:** Widely planted in U.S.

COMMON JUNIPER
Juniperus communis

Y ou're more likely to see this species growing as a shrub than a tree. It can reach 50 feet in height, but usually grows only 12 to 48 inches tall. Common Junipers are the most widespread conifer in the world, growing in North America, Europe, and Asia—even in Iceland and Greenland. Very few trees grow naturally in both the Old and New Worlds. Junipers offer abundant food and excellent shelter for deer and numerous songbirds and game birds.

Look for: A clumpy shrub or small tree. Sharp needles ¼–1" long and 3-sided, in bundles of three. Blackish-blue cones with a white, powdery covering; look like berries.

Shape and Height: Wide-spreading; usually 12–48".

Habitat: Rocky, infertile soils in mountains and pastures.

Range: Throughout Canada and widespread in northern and western U.S.

Eastern Red Cedar
Juniperus virginiana

Look for: A conifer with two types of needles: small, scalelike, and blunt on older parts of tree; long and sharp on young twigs. Blue-green, berrylike cones have whitish, waxy covering. Bark reddish and shreddy. **Shape and Height:** Triangular; to 50'. **Habitat:** Rocky, infertile soils, especially in abandoned pastures. **Range:** Eastern U.S.

Incense Cedar
Libocedrus decurrens

Look for: A very aromatic conifer. Blue-green, 1"-long needles lie flat, are very fragrant when crushed. Reddish-brown 1"-long cones. Shredding, reddish bark with deep furrows. Commonly grows in Giant Sequoia groves. **Shape and Height:** Oval; to 150'. **Habitat:** Moist to dry soils in mountains. **Range:** Parts of Oregon, California, and Nevada.

CONES

59

CALIFORNIA FAN PALM
Washingtonia filifera

The desert oases of Southern California and nearby Arizona are the true native homes of the California Fan Palm, but you don't have to visit an oasis to see one of these handsome trees. Many southwestern towns have them planted along their main streets. The California towns of Twentynine Palms and Palm Springs were named for this tree.

Look for: Fan-shaped leaves 3–6' wide, split into many leaflets; leafstalk lined with thorns. Clusters of ¼"-long blue-black fruits. Trunk thickly covered with dead leaves.

Shape and Height: Fan-shaped; to 80'.

Habitat: Deserts; also planted in urban areas.

Range: Southern California and western Arizona.

Caution: Leaves are prickly.

Cabbage Palmetto
Sabal palmetto

Look for: Enormous leaves 5–8' long, with 6'-long, half-rounded stalks. Clusters of small white flowers become ¼"-long blackish fruits. A crisscross pattern of old leaf stems on younger palm trunks; older trunks are gray and smooth. Trunk width equal throughout its length. **Shape and Height:** Fan-shaped; to 80'. **Habitat:** Inland hills and sandy shores. **Range:** Atlantic and Gulf coasts of southeastern U.S.

Coconut Palm
Cocos nucifera

Look for: A smooth grayish trunk, straight or gently curving. Feathery leaves up to 18' long. Fruit enclosed in large brown husk. Coconut Palms have been growing in North America for centuries but aren't native. **Shape and Height:** Fan-shaped; to 100'. **Habitat:** Near coastal areas. **Range:** Southern Florida.

Yuccas are odd-shaped, fascinating members of the agave family, often mistaken for cactuses. The Joshua Tree is the largest of the yuccas by far, though it has the shortest leaves. It grows remarkably slowly and lives in one of the hottest, driest climates on the continent. If you find yourself in California's Joshua Tree National Park, home to the best stands of Joshua Trees, look for the white Yucca Moths that pollinate yucca blossoms in the evening.

Look for: Upward-curving branches covered with leaves. Green leaves 8–12" long, very narrow, and armed with small "teeth." Blossoms March–May with 2" whitish flowers in foot-long clusters. Fruits oblong, podlike, and brown.

Shape and Height: Irregular; to 30'.

Habitat: Gentle desert slopes.

Range: Southwestern U.S.

Caution: Leaves are prickly.

Soaptree
Yucca elata

Look for: A small tree with 12"- to 30"-long prickly, pale yellow-green leaves that are smooth, flexible, and narrow (only ¼" wide). White flowers bloom from May to July on 3'- to 6'-long stalks in attractive clusters. Fruits are brown and podlike. **Shape and Height:** Oval; usually 6', but can grow to 20'. **Habitat:** Dry soils in grasslands and deserts. **Range:** Southwestern U.S.

Aloe Yucca
Yucca aloifolia

Look for: A typical yucca with long, narrow leaves and projecting flower/fruit clusters. Narrow, dark green leaves 18–30" long. Flowers in clusters 8–24" long. Fruit 4" long, ripens from green to black. **Shape and Height:** Oval; to 25'. **Habitat:** Dry soils in coastal areas. **Range:** Atlantic and Gulf coasts of southeastern U.S.

63

PUSSY WILLOW
Salix discolor

Other willows may brighten the springtime landscape with their long yellow-green twigs and graceful forms, but the Pussy Willow enchants us with its silvery, furry catkins, called "pussies." People young and old snip off the spring branchlets, filled with catkins, and bring some springtime into their homes. Wait too long and the silver will have turned to gold.

LOOK FOR: A small, usually shrubby tree. Blue-green leaves 2–5" long, pointed, toothed, and whitish beneath. Purplish twigs with furry catkins on male plants in early spring.

SHAPE AND HEIGHT: Round; to 25'.

HABITAT: Riverbanks and other moist soils; also some drier soils.

RANGE: Southern Canada and northeastern U.S.; spotty in western U.S.

PACIFIC WILLOW
Salix lasiandra

LOOK FOR: Leaves 3–6" long and ½–¾" wide, pointy, toothed, shiny, dark green above and paler beneath. A spreading tree or shrub with furrowed, dark gray bark. A very common tree along rivers in the Pacific Northwest. **SHAPE AND HEIGHT:** Wide-spreading; to 50'. **HABITAT:** Moist soils in northern and western mountains. **RANGE:** Western Canada and U.S.

BLACK WILLOW
Salix nigra

LOOK FOR: A large, spreading willow. New twigs light greenish-yellow in winter and springtime. New saplings take root from discarded twigs. Similar to the Pacific Willow, with dark, furrowed bark but with narrower, lighter leaves. **SHAPE AND HEIGHT:** Wide-spreading; to 40'. **HABITAT:** Banks of rivers, lakes, and streams. **RANGE:** Eastern U.S., California, and southwestern U.S.

CATKINS

65

QUAKING ASPEN
Populus tremuloides

LEAF

Looks can be deceiving. Brightly colored aspen trees, waving their brilliant summer-green or autumn-gold leaves back and forth in the slightest breeze, seem delicate and light. The aspens that make up handsome aspen groves are actually one enormous plant per grove. Each aspen sends up shoots from its roots to make other trunks, the new trunks do the same, and eventually the grove is gigantic.

Look for: The most widespread tree in North America. Grows in groves; easy to identify. Leaves 1½–3" long, rounded, with coarse teeth and a pointed tip; turn golden yellow in fall. Leafstalks are flat, causing leaves to flutter in light wind. Smooth, light greenish-gray bark.

Shape and Height: Oval; to 60'.

Habitat: Moist soils in open areas; higher elevations in the West.

Range: Most of Canada, Alaska, and western and northeastern U.S.

Eastern Cottonwood
Populus deltoides

Look for: Triangular leaves 2–8" long, coarse-toothed, turn yellow. Female flowers have seeds with cottony threads that cover the ground beneath the trees and give the tree its name. Trunk with dark gray, ridged bark. Common in prairie states. **Shape and Height:** Oval; to 100'. **Habitat:** Moist soils, often along streams. **Range:** Alberta and south to Texas and much of eastern U.S.

Black Cottonwood
Populus trichocarpa

Look for: Largest broadleaf tree of the Pacific Northwest. Triangular leaves 4–8" long, sharply pointed, dark green above and silvery beneath, turn yellow. Older trees have blackish trunks with deeply furrowed bark. **Shape and Height:** Oval; to 180'. **Habitat:** Moist soils, often along riverbanks. **Range:** Alaska to California and in northern Rocky Mts.

SOUTHERN BAYBERRY
Myrica cerifera

FRUITS

Bayberries most often grow as shrubs in nature—very seldom do we sit under a bayberry and enjoy its shade. The Southern Bayberry (also known as the Wax Myrtle) is covered in fall and winter with waxy, light blue berries, which are a reliable food source for songbirds. Candlemakers use the wax coatings of the berries to make sweet-smelling candles.

LOOK FOR: A shrub or small tree that often grows in thickets. Evergreen leaves 2–4" long, coarse-toothed, shiny green above and orange-brown beneath.

SHAPE AND HEIGHT: Round; to 40', usually much shorter.

HABITAT: Damp, sandy soils in open areas.

RANGE: Southeastern U.S.

NORTHERN BAYBERRY
Myrica pensylvanica

LOOK FOR: A shrub or small tree, very similar to Southern Bayberry but ranging far to the north. Aromatic leaves stay green, fall late in the year. Distinctive light gray-blue, waxy berries. The Yellow-rumped Warbler relishes the berries and is often found eating in bayberry thickets.
SHAPE AND HEIGHT: Round; to 35'; usually much shorter. **HABITAT:** Infertile, sandy soils in open areas. **RANGE:** Newfoundland to eastern U.S.

PACIFIC BAYBERRY
Myrica californica

LOOK FOR: Shrub or small tree that often grows in thickets. Aromatic evergreen leaves 3–4" long and ½–1" wide, with coarse teeth. Dark purple fruit with whitish, waxy coating. **SHAPE AND HEIGHT:** Round; 20–30' as a tree, usually a shrub. **HABITAT:** Sand dunes and hillsides at low elevations. **RANGE:** Pacific Coast of U.S.

BLACK WALNUT

Juglans nigra

Black Walnuts used to be more common than they are today, but untold numbers were cut down during World Wars I and II to get wood for making guns. You can still find these trees over a large range of the East, and they are worth looking for. The big green nut husks are the giveaway on the Black Walnut, which sheds its leaves early so everyone can appreciate its fruit. Be careful— walnut husks will dye your hands dark brown.

Look for: Compound leaves 8–24" long, with 15–23 leaflets (each 2–4" long and toothed) that turn yellow. Green-husked 2", round fruits on tree and scattered on ground below. Dark brown to blackish, furrowed bark.

Shape and Height: Oval; to 100'.

Habitat: Fertile soils in woods.

Range: Eastern U.S. to Great Plains.

ARIZONA WALNUT
Juglans major

Look for: Compound leaves with 9–15 toothed leaflets, each 2–4" long. Deeply grooved nuts inside 1–1½", round, light brown husks. Deeply furrowed brown bark. **Shape and Height:** Wide-spreading; to 50'. **Habitat:** Mountain valleys at high altitudes; widely planted as an ornamental tree. **Range:** Southwestern U.S.

ENGLISH WALNUT
Juglans regia

Look for: A walnut tree similar to Black Walnut, but with shorter leaves and only 7–9 leaflets. Large nuts are thin-shelled with green husks. The familiar walnuts in stores. **Shape and Height:** Wide-spreading; to 70'. **Habitat:** Fertile soils in orchards and residential areas. **Range:** Widely planted in U.S., especially in Oregon and California.

SHAGBARK HICKORY
Carya ovata

The great shags of bark that separate from the trunk at the bottom and top, which give this tree its wonderful appearance, are not signs that the tree is falling apart at the seams. In fact, Shagbark Hickory wood is stronger than steel. The shaggy bark may prevent some mammals from climbing up the trunk and eating all the delicious nuts. After all, the bark doesn't get really shaggy until the tree is old enough to make nuts.

LOOK FOR: Compound leaves 8–12" long, with 5 (sometimes 7–9) large leaflets; turn golden in fall. Nut inside 1"- to 2½"-long brown husk, which splits open when the nut is ripe (walnut husks do not split open). Gray bark on older trees loosens into shaggy strips, up to 4' long.

SHAPE AND HEIGHT: Oval; to 90'.

HABITAT: Moist soils on hillsides and near streams.

RANGE: Eastern U.S.

PIGNUT HICKORY
Carya glabra

LOOK FOR: Compound leaves 8–12" long, with 3–7 (usually 5) leaflets, each 2–3½" long. Greenish-brown nut husks are pear-shaped and split open when ripe. Nuts can be bitter, and are often left on the ground by farmers for their pigs to eat. Bark is smooth and gray. **SHAPE AND HEIGHT:** Oval; to 75'. **HABITAT:** Dry soils in woods. **RANGE:** Eastern U.S.

PECAN
Carya illinoensis

LOOK FOR: Compound leaves 12–20" long, with 11–17 toothed leaflets that turn yellow. Light brown, 1"- to 2"-long nuts inside oval brown husks. Bark is light gray-brown. The most valuable crop tree in America; often planted in groves. **SHAPE AND HEIGHT:** Vase-shaped; to 100'. **HABITAT:** Rich soils near lowland rivers and streams. **RANGE:** Southeastern U.S.

PAPER BIRCH
Betula papyrifera

A lso called "Canoe Birch" and "White Birch," this beautiful tree got its names from the different features of its bark. Thin, lightweight, waterproof, and the whitest in color of any tree bark, the bark of the Paper Birch was sometimes used as paper by early settlers. It was also perfect for covering canoes. Since Paper Birch bark grows in numerous thin layers, the air trapped between the layers of bark makes great insulation for this northern tree.

LOOK FOR: A tree with a white trunk with thin, black horizontal lines; light orange inner bark seen where outer bark has been peeled away. Green leaves 2–3" long, oval, pointed, and toothed; turn yellow in fall. Often grows in groves.

SHAPE AND HEIGHT: Oval; to 80'.

HABITAT: Many soil types in woods and openings.

RANGE: Alaska, most of Canada, and northern U.S.

WATER BIRCH
Betula occidentalis

LOOK FOR: Leaves 1–3" long, dark green above and lighter beneath, with toothed edges; turn yellow in fall. Shiny, nonpeeling reddish-brown bark with horizontal, whitish lines. Often grows in groves. **SHAPE AND HEIGHT:** Oval; to 25'. **HABITAT:** Moist soils, especially along streams. **RANGE:** Southwestern Canada and western U.S.

GRAY BIRCH
Betula populifolia

LOOK FOR: A small tree often mistaken for Paper Birch. Dull gray-white bark with horizontal black markings, never as clear white as Paper Birch and not orange underneath. Sharply triangular leaves 2–3" long, dark green above and lighter beneath; turn yellow in fall. **SHAPE AND HEIGHT:** Oval; to 30'. **HABITAT:** Infertile soils, especially in abandoned fields. **RANGE:** Eastern Canada and northeastern U.S.

RED ALDER
Alnus rubra

LEAVES AND CATKINS

This is the most common broadleaf of the Northwest. It is a pioneer tree that pops up everywhere in the wake of fires and land clearings and takes over the land until larger species overgrow it. Many alders grow mainly as shrubs, but the Red Alder grows to a fine tree size. Alders have female catkins that look like little brown cones, making them easy to identify throughout the year. American Beavers, Mountain Beavers, and Common Porcupines eat catkins.

LOOK FOR: Oval leaves 3–6" long, dark green and smooth on top, lighter and rust-colored beneath, toothed with curled-under edges. Female "cones" are ½–1" long. Male catkins to 5" long. Trunk with white-splotched gray bark. Often grows in groves.

SHAPE AND HEIGHT: Oval; to 80'.

HABITAT: Open areas, especially cut-over or burned areas and along rivers.

RANGE: Pacific Coast from Alaska to California, and Idaho.

MOUNTAIN ALDER
Alnus tenuifolia

LOOK FOR: A shrub or small tree with oval leaves 1–3" long, fine-toothed and not rolled under. Cones about ½" long, smaller than Red Alder's. Bark is gray or brown.
SHAPE AND HEIGHT: Vase-shaped; to 30', usually a shorter shrub. **HABITAT:** Moist, cool soils in mountains. **RANGE:** Alaska, western Canada, and western U.S.

SPECKLED ALDER
Alnus rugosa

LOOK FOR: Leaves 2–5" long, wavy-edged, and toothed. Cones ¼–½" long. Brown to gray, smooth bark with horizontal, whitish marks. **SHAPE AND HEIGHT:** Wide-spreading; to 30', though usually a shrub to 10'. **HABITAT:** Moist soils, especially along streams and rivers. **RANGE:** Most of Canada and northeastern U.S.

AMERICAN HORNBEAM
Carpinus caroliniana

BARK

If you want to look at a tough tree, check out an American Hornbeam. The bark is smooth and looks as if it's bulging with muscles. In fact, the tight, muscular look and feel of the tree is its outstanding field mark. This tree not only looks tough, it is. The pioneers called it "Ironwood" because they dulled their saws and axes trying to cut the extremely hard wood. The name "hornbeam" comes from two old-time words: "horn" for tough and "beam" for tree.

Look for: Toothed leaves resembling birch leaves, 2–4" long, blue-green above, paler beneath; turn orange to red. Has smooth, "muscular" blue-gray bark.

Shape and Height: Vase-shaped; to 40'.

Habitat: Moist soils, especially near streams and swamps.

Range: Eastern half of U.S.

LEAVES AND FRUITS

EASTERN HOP HORNBEAM
Ostrya virginiana

Look for: A small tree with oblong yellow-green leaves, 3–5" long, soft, fine-toothed; turn yellow in fall. Fruits resemble common hops (small, flat, brown, oval nutlets) in 1½"- to 2"-long clusters that hang down like cones. Each saclike fruit contains a single seed, which is unusual for fruits. Reddish-gray bark with narrow, shredding strips. **Shape and Height:** Oval; to 30'. **Habitat:** Dry soils in woods. **Range:** Eastern half of U.S.

TRUNK

79

AMERICAN BEECH
Fagus grandifolia

Even before Daniel Boone carved his famous message, "D Boone cilled a bar on tree in year 1760," people carved their initials (and quite often those of a loved one) upon the smooth, silvery bark of the American Beech. Beech trees can survive these gouges (Daniel Boone's tree lived to be 365 years old) as long as the bark is not cut all around the tree. Beech bark is elastic and alive, stretching instead of cracking as the tree grows.

Look for: Sharp-pointed, toothed leaves 2–6" long; green in summer, golden in fall, whitish in winter (when some cling to the tree). Triangular beechnuts, edible to wildlife and humans, are brown, with prickly husks. Bark is smooth and gray.

Shape and Height: Oval; to 100'.

Habitat: Moist, rich soils in woods.

Range: Southeastern Canada and most of eastern half of U.S.

AMERICAN CHESTNUT
Castanea dentata

Look for: Shiny green leaves 5–8" long, edged with forward-pointing teeth; turn yellow in fall. Unfortunately, now most often seen as a dead trunk, often with sprouts growing from roots. Once a major tree of the East, it was almost completely destroyed by a fungal disease that was introduced to the environment. **Shape and Height:** Oval; originally to 100', now seldom more than 20'. **Habitat:** Rich soils in woods. **Range:** Eastern U.S.

GIANT CHINKAPIN "GOLDEN CHINKAPIN"
Castanopsis chrysophylla

Look for: Interesting-looking tree with chestnutlike fruit. Evergreen leaves 2–5" long, dark green above and golden below. Round, prickly husks 1–1½" wide; contain 1 or 2 small edible nuts. **Shape and Height:** Oval; to 100'. **Habitat:** Mountain forests. **Range:** Oregon and California.

WHITE OAK
Quercus alba

LEAVES

The White Oak has two important distinctions. First, its light-colored, beautifully grained, slow-burning wood makes it the all-American number one choice of woodworkers, lumbermen, and fire stokers. Second, its foliage makes it number one in the caterpillar world—more kinds of caterpillars feed on White Oak leaves than on any other known plant.

LOOK FOR: Branches of mature oak may spread 125' across. Bright green leaves 5–8" long, with many rounded lobes; turn red to brown in fall. Flowers on catkins. Acorns ½–¾" long, set in small cups. Acorns are plentiful from all oaks and are an important food source to many wildlife. Bark is light gray.

SHAPE AND HEIGHT: Wide-spreading; to 100'.

HABITAT: Variety of soils in lowlands and on lower slopes.

RANGE: Eastern U.S.

BUR OAK
Quercus macrocarpa

LOOK FOR: A tree similar to White Oak, but with shaggy acorns and most abundant in the Midwest. Leaves 6–12" long, with many lobes (widest at center); turn yellow to brown in fall. Acorns ¾–2" long inside deep cups with gray, hairlike covering.
SHAPE AND HEIGHT: Wide-spreading; to 80'.
HABITAT: Near lowland rivers and streams.
RANGE: Central Canada and U.S. south to Texas.

LIVE OAK
Quercus virginiana

LOOK FOR: An evergreen oak with long, huge horizontal limbs. Oval, unlobed leaves 2–4" long, shiny dark green above and silvery green below. Acorns 1" long, rich brown, slender. One of the showcase trees of the South. Sometimes forms thickets.
SHAPE AND HEIGHT: Wide-spreading with huge crown; to 50'. **HABITAT:** Mostly lowlands.
RANGE: Southeastern U.S.

NORTHERN RED OAK
Quercus rubra

It is said that if a parachutist jumped from a plane over the Northeast and landed in a tree, that tree would most likely be an oak, and probably a Northern Red Oak. This is a very common tree, indeed, but since it is both a handsome species and a fast grower, folks can't get enough of it and plant it in parks and along town streets.

Look for: Leaves 5–8" long and 4–5" wide, with 7–11 toothed, pointed lobes, green above and paler beneath; turn red to brown in fall. Acorns 1½" long with shallow cups. Brownish-black bark with deep ridges.

Shape and Height: Oval; to 70'.

Habitat: Rich or sandy soils at many elevations.

Range: Eastern Canada and U.S.

LEAVES

Black Oak
Quercus velutina

Look for: Leaves similar to Northern Red Oak, but usually only 5–7 lobes and noticeably hairy beneath (smooth in Northern Red Oak); turn red to brown in fall. Acorns ½–¾" long, with yellow nut meat and yellow-lined cups. **Shape and Height:** Oval; to 70'. **Habitat:** Dry soils in lowlands and hills. **Range:** Eastern U.S.

Blackjack Oak
Quercus marilandica

Look for: A crooked, scrubby oak, shaped like a kite. Leathery leaves 3–5" long, shiny above and brownish and hairy beneath; turn yellow to brown in fall. Acorns ¾" long, half covered by cups. Bark is thick and blackish. **Shape and Height:** Wide-spreading; to 40'. **Habitat:** Sandy soils in open areas. **Range:** Mid-Atlantic and southeastern U.S.

85

VALLEY OAK
Quercus lobata

LEAVES

Twenty-one kinds of oaks live in California. Twelve are mostly shrubby, while nine are always tree-sized. The biggest of California's oaks, in fact one of the tallest of all American oaks, is the Valley Oak. It can live to be 600 years old! True to its name, it grows in the San Joaquin and Sacramento valleys, spreading its enormous limbs outward and upward over the fertile valley.

CANYON LIVE OAK
Quercus chrysolepis

LOOK FOR: An oak with massive limbs. Oval evergreen leaves 1–4" long, with smooth edges, shiny green above and yellowish beneath. Acorns ½–1" long with golden, woolly cups. Bark is black. **SHAPE AND HEIGHT:** Wide-spreading; to 80', often only a shrub. **HABITAT:** Rocky canyons. **RANGE:** Oregon to Arizona.

COAST LIVE OAK
Quercus agrifolia

LOOK FOR: An oak with wide-spreading side branches almost touching ground. Oval evergreen leaves 1–3" long, shiny green above, and arching like little umbrellas. Chestnut-brown acorns 1–1½" long, slim and pointed. Major tree along the coast of California from San Francisco southward. **SHAPE AND HEIGHT:** Wide-spreading; to 90'. **HABITAT:** Valleys and grasslands. **RANGE:** Coast of California.

LOOK FOR: A large oak with long, thick, drooping limbs. Leaves 2–4" long with 7–9 rounded lobes. Chestnut-brown acorns, 1–2¼" long, have small pebbly cups. Bark is gray-brown and well furrowed.

SHAPE AND HEIGHT: Wide-spreading; to 120'.

HABITAT: Fertile soils in valleys.

RANGE: Coast Ranges and Sierra Nevada in California.

87

AMERICAN ELM
Ulmus americana

LEAF

Like the American Chestnut, many American Elms have been destroyed by fungal diseases that were accidentally introduced to America in the 20th century. Dutch Elm disease is spread by the Elm Bark Beetle, which obviously gets around. Most of the stately, fountainlike elms that graced main streets and town squares of so many New England towns have died from the dreaded disease.

Look for: Unique vase shape, with main trunk dividing into several trunks close to the ground. Dark green, pointed leaves 4–6" long, toothed, sandpapery, lopsided at the base; turn yellow in fall. Waferlike fruits ½" long, greenish-brown; ripen in spring. Cross section of bark shows distinctive light and dark layers.

Shape and Height: Vase-shaped; to 120'.

Habitat: Near lowland rivers and streams and in towns.

Range: Southern Canada, Great Plains, and eastern U.S.

SIBERIAN ELM
Ulmus pumila

Look for : A very fast-growing tree widely planted in the Great Plains states for windbreaks and for decoration on town streets. Dark green leaves 1–3" long, narrow, toothed (even at base); turn yellow in fall. Native to Siberia and northern. China. Resistant to Dutch Elm disease. **Shape and Height:** Wide-spreading; to 40'. **Habitat:** Moist soils along hedges and in towns. **Range:** Planted in central and western U.S.

HACKBERRY
Celtis occidentalis

Look for: Thin green leaves 3–5" long, toothed, lopsided at the base; turn yellow in fall. Dark purple berries hang singly from twig ends. Gray-brown bark with distinctive corky lumps. Several butterflies, including the Hackberry Emperor, may be seen nearby. **Shape and Height:** Wide-spreading; to 70'. **Habitat:** Streamsides. **Range:** North-central and northeastern U.S.

RED MULBERRY
Morus rubra

FRUITS

People who make special trips to collect blackberries and raspberries may never think about gathering the juicy fruits of the Red Mulberry. But look at how the birds love them. Baltimore Orioles, Rose-breasted Grosbeaks, and other colorful songbirds enjoy eating fruits from mulberry trees—they are just about the best natural bird feeders. Once you are sure you have the right species, give these fruits a try and see what the birds have been enjoying all these years.

Look for: A straight tree with dark green leaves 3–5" long, toothed and rounded, usually with 1–2 curved lobes, coarse top surface; turn yellow in fall. Fruits blackish-purple when ripe. Bark is dark reddish-brown.

Shape and Height: Wide-spreading; to 70'.

Habitat: Fertile, moist soils.

Range: Eastern U.S.

WHITE MULBERRY
Morus alba

Look for: Shiny green leaves 3–10" long, smooth and toothed, usually with 3–5 uneven lobes; turn yellow in fall. Whitish to purple fruits are eaten by birds throughout the summer. Bark is yellow-brown. A native tree of China, in the past many White Mulberries were planted to provide leaves for silkworms. **Shape and Height:** Oval; to 60'. **Habitat:** Variety of soils in parks and woods. **Range:** Eastern U.S. and parts of California and Washington.

BLACK MULBERRY
Morus nigra

Look for: A tree very similar to Red Mulberry, but leaves rarely lobed. Dark green, heart-shaped leaves, 3–5" long; turn yellow in fall. Fruits large, edible, and black when ripe. **Shape and Height:** Wide-spreading; to 50'. **Habitat:** Mainly cultivated areas, such as parks and yards. **Range:** Southeastern U.S.

For sheer flower power, it's hard to top the magnolias. The Southern Magnolia, a well-known symbol of the South, is the grandest of them all. From late spring until early summer, the huge, fragrant white blossoms decorate the fine, dark, glossy foliage. Later in the season, you'll see small red seeds hanging from 4"-long podlike fruiting structures where the flowers blossomed earlier. This showy tree is planted in warm climates around the world.

Look for: Evergreen leaves 5–8" long, thick, oval, shiny above and rusty and hairy beneath. White flowers 6–8" long. Scaly gray-brown bark.

Shape and Height: Oval or triangular; to 80'.

Habitat: Moist soils in woodland understories.

Range: Southeastern U.S.; planted in coastal California.

FLOWER

Cucumber Tree
"Cucumber Magnolia"
Magnolia acuminata

Look for: Yellow-green leaves 6–10" long, broad and pointed. Light yellow-green flowers 2" long. Fruit up to 3" long, 1" around; looks like small reddish-brown cucumber in shape. Scaly gray-brown bark. **Shape and Height:** Triangular; to 90'. **Habitat:** Fertile soils around bases of mountains. **Range:** New York to Louisiana (inland).

Tulip Tree
"Yellow Poplar"
Liriodendron tulipifera

Look for: The tallest, straightest American broadleaf. Tulip-shaped leaves 6–10" long; turn yellow in fall. Tulip-shaped light green flowers with orange bases, 1–2" long; bloom from May–June; may be too high up to be noticed. Also known as Yellow Poplar, but not a true poplar. **Shape and Height:** Oval; to 150'. **Habitat:** Moist soils in woods. **Range:** Eastern U.S.; planted on Pacific Coast of U.S.

93

SASSAFRAS
Sassafras albidum

THREE LEAF SHAPES

Sassafras trees are a delight to the senses. Their leaves have an aromatic sweetness when crushed. Their roots (the original source of root beer) smell exactly like the soda when twisted to release their sap. The leaves come in three shapes—most easily remembered as the shapes of footballs, mittens, and ghosts. You may see all three shapes on one branch. In fall, it is hard not to notice the brilliant, deep blue fruits on their deep red stalks.

Look for: Usually a small, open tree. Dark green leaves 4–6" long, shiny above and lighter beneath, in 3 basic shapes; turn yellow, orange, or red in fall.

Shape and Height: Oval; to 50', often grows as a much shorter shrub.

Habitat: Moist, sandy soils on edges and in understories of forests.

Range: Eastern U.S.

California Laurel
Umbellularia californica

Look for: Leathery evergreen leaves shiny green above and paler beneath, 3–5" long, smooth-edged; very spicy when crushed. Green to purplish fruits ¾–1" long, appear in fall. Greenish-brown bark on short, wide trunk. One of the most handsome West Coast trees; often called Oregon Myrtle in Oregon. **Shape and Height:** Oval; to 60', usually a shrub. **Habitat:** Fertile soils along coast and on lower slopes. **Range:** Oregon and California.

Redbay
Persea borbonia

Look for: Evergreen leaves 3–4" long, shiny green above and lighter beneath, smooth-edged, aromatic. Leaves used as herbs. Small yellowish-white flowers grow into ½", deep purple, spherical fruits. **Shape and Height:** Oval; to 60'. **Habitat:** Moist soils, especially along streams or in swamps. **Range:** Coast of southeastern U.S.

SWEETGUM
Liquidambar styraciflua

LEAVES AND FRUIT

Sweetgum gets its common and scientific names from the thick, gummy sap that oozes from a broken spot on the tree. It can be chewed like gum and looks like liquid amber. Sweetgums are most easily recognized by the round, prickly fruits that hang from their twigs like ornaments through the winter. In fact, these "balls" are often collected and used for making Christmas decorations. One of the most common large trees in the mid-South and common as a shade tree in the Ohio River Valley.

LOOK FOR: A tall tree with twigs that have corky ridges. Star-shaped, shiny green leaves 5–8" long, with 5–7 toothed and triangular lobes; turn red in fall. Prickly fruits on long-stemmed, hanging spheres. Has furrowed gray bark.

SHAPE AND HEIGHT: Oval; to 120'.

HABITAT: Rich soils in swampy areas.

RANGE: Most of eastern U.S.; planted in California.

WITCH HAZEL
Hamamelis virginiana

LOOK FOR: A small tree, about as wide across as it is tall. Leaves 2–6" long, wavy-edged and rough-toothed; turn yellow in fall. Flowers yellow and ribbonlike. Small seed capsules are hard, dark brown, and stay on tree through the year. Before the flowers open, the seeds shoot up to 30' from their capsules. Flowers bloom in mid-fall. Hairy yellow-gray bark. **SHAPE AND HEIGHT:** Round; to 30', usually a 10'- to 12'-high shrub. **HABITAT:** Moist soils, often near streams. **RANGE:** Eastern Canada and U.S.

FLOWERS

97

AMERICAN SYCAMORE
Platanus occidentalis

LEAVES AND FRUITS

The sycamores are commonly known as "planetrees" in other parts of the world. They are immediately recognized by their bark, which looks like a gray, white, greenish, and purplish patchwork to some and like army camouflage to others. The American Sycamore is the most massive tree in eastern North America and can have an enormous trunk. Early pioneers used hollow sycamores for sheds, animal shelters, and even temporary housing for themselves. Trees 15 feet in diameter have been found.

LOOK FOR: Leaves 4–8" long and wide; shaped like maple leaves, but wider and with shallower lobes; turn brown in fall. Fruits are round, 1–1½" balls of brown seeds that hang alone on long stems. Tan, gray, white, and greenish bark in loose plates.

SHAPE AND HEIGHT: Oval; usually to 100', have been known to grow to 200'.

HABITAT: Moist soils; common along streams.

RANGE: Eastern U.S.

CALIFORNIA SYCAMORE
Platanus racemosa

LOOK FOR: A wide-spreading, crooked-limbed tree. Leaves up to 10" wide, very maplelike. Seed balls hang in groups of three to seven. Crown spread known to be 150' wide. Has typical sycamore bark pattern. **SHAPE AND HEIGHT:** Vase-shaped; to 90'. **HABITAT:** Moist soils along streams. **RANGE:** California.

LONDON PLANETREE
Platanus x acerifolia

LOOK FOR: Shiny green leaves 5–10" long and wide, 3–5 lobes, with few or no teeth. Two fruit balls per stalk (only one on American Sycamore). Trunk similar to American, but bark has yellowish patches, not white. A hybrid, or mixed, species of Eastern Sycamore and Oriental Planetree. **SHAPE AND HEIGHT:** Oval; to 70'. **HABITAT:** Planted along streets and in parks. **RANGE:** Widely planted across U.S.

COMMON APPLE
Malus sylvestris

FLOWERS

The apple tree is a year-round source of delight. Springtime brings beautiful white flowers. In summer there's bright foliage. The delicious fruits are ripe in the fall. During the winter, nutritious buds from the tree are food for game birds. Partridges like apple (not pear) trees. The apple is not a native species, but was brought to North America by early settlers. About 3,000 varieties of apples have been cultivated in North America.

LOOK FOR: Oval leaves, 1–2" long, toothed; turn green-brown in fall. Flowers white to pinkish, 1¼" wide, in small clusters. Apples 2–3½" wide, attached by short, thick twigs (necessary to hold the heavy apples). Has a short trunk with gray bark.

SHAPE AND HEIGHT: Round; to 30'.

HABITAT: Many soil types in orchards, old farmlands, and towns.

RANGE: Native to Old World but naturalized widely in North America.

OREGON CRABAPPLE
Malus fusca

LOOK FOR: A small tree or shrub that sometimes forms thickets. Oval, shiny green leaves 1–4" long, sharply toothed; turn orange to red in fall. Clusters of white flowers, about 1" wide, from May–June. Oblong fruits ¼–¾" long, become dark red Aug.–Sept. **SHAPE AND HEIGHT:** Round; to 40'. **HABITAT:** Moist soils. **RANGE:** Pacific Coast from Alaska to California.

AMERICAN MOUNTAIN ASH
Sorbus americana

LOOK FOR: Compound leaves 6–9" long, with 13–17 blue-green, slim, toothed leaflets; turn yellow in fall. Small, white or pink, flat-topped clusters of flowers develop into round, bright orange-red ¼" berries, which usually stay on the tree until eaten by birds. Smooth gray bark. Apples and mountain ashes are in the rose family. **SHAPE AND HEIGHT:** Oval; to 30'. **HABITAT:** Rocky hillsides; widely planted. **RANGE:** Southeastern Canada and northeastern U.S.

101

COMMON CHOKECHERRY
Prunus virginiana

FRUITS

Chokecherries, whether growing under aspens in the West or in a scraggly abandoned pasture in the East, attract a lot of attention from wild creatures. Birds, especially, love the cherries, and it is a common sight to see bluebirds, robins, waxwings, and grosbeaks enjoying the fruits. Tent caterpillars and webworms build their silken webs in cherry and apple trees. This species is one of the most widespread of American trees. Its fruits can be made into jams and jellies.

Look for: A small, twisted tree; may form thickets. Oval leaves, 2–5" long, sharp-toothed; turn yellow in fall. Small white flowers, in 3"- to 6"-long dangling clusters, April–July. Blackish-red cherries Aug.–Oct. Bark is gray-brown.

Shape and Height: Oval; to 25'.

Habitat: Many soil types.

Range: Southern Canada and western and northern U.S.

BITTER CHERRY
Prunus emarginata

Look for: A small tree that may grow in thickets. Blunt-toothed leaves with rounded tips, 1–3" long. White flowers ½" wide in clusters of 6 to 12. Red to black fruits are very bitter, but eaten by birds and mammals. The smooth reddish-brown bark is marked with light horizontal lines.
Shape and Height: Oval; to 40'. **Habitat:** Moist soils. **Range:** Southwestern Canada and western U.S.

BLACK CHERRY
Prunus serotina

Look for: Shiny green leaves 2–6" long, pointed, sharp-toothed; turn yellow to red in fall. Small white flowers in drooping clusters, with dark purple cherries 2 months later. Beautiful wood in larger specimens. Mature tree has black, scaly bark; younger tree has smooth reddish-brown bark marked with white horizontal lines. **Shape and Height:** Oval; to 60'. **Habitat:** Deep, moist or sandy soils in woods. **Range:** Eastern Canada and U.S. and parts of southwestern U.S.

103

AMERICAN PLUM
Prunus americana

FLOWERS

In spring, a thicket of American Plums with their spreading branches filled with beautiful white flowers is a sight to see. You may not want to get too close, however, because the flowers have a rather sickening smell. Wild plum fruits are very sour and seldom eaten raw by humans or wild animals, though foxes are known to enjoy them.

Look for: A small tree with wide-spreading, somewhat drooping branches; forms thickets along streams. Leaves 1–5" long, sharp-toothed and narrowing to a point. Flowers 1" wide, in clusters of three to five, April–June. Red or yellow plums, ¾–1" wide, round; ripe in fall. Thorns on branchlets.

Shape and Height: Wide-spreading; to 30'; often much shorter or a shrub.

Habitat: Moist soils.

Range: Central and eastern U.S.

KLAMATH PLUM
Prunus subcordata

Look for: A small tree with a rounded crown. Leaves egg-shaped to nearly round, 1–3" long, fine-toothed, turn yellow to red. White flowers ¾" wide in clusters of three to four. Plums ¼–1" wide, round, sour, mostly bright red. Bark is gray-brown. **Shape and Height:** Oval; to 25'. **Habitat:** Rocky slopes; to 6,000' in Coast Ranges and Sierra Nevada. **Range:** Oregon and California.

CHICKASAW PLUM
Prunus angustifolia

Look for: A small tree or thicket-forming shrub. Shiny fine-toothed leaves, 1–3" long, about ⅓ as wide. White flowers ½" wide in small clusters. Plums ½" wide, round, red to yellow, ripe in late summer. **Shape and Height:** Round; to 25'. **Habitat:** Moist soils along roads and in open areas. **Range:** Southeastern U.S.

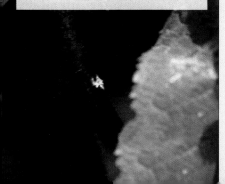

BLACK HAWTHORN
Crataegus douglasii

FLOWERS

Some trees are made for climbing, but not the hawthorns, which are armed with wicked thorns on tangled branches. Many species of birds love to nest in hawthorns because this thorny protection keeps people and predators away from their nestlings. Black Hawthorn is one of many North American hawthorns. It is the most widespread western hawthorn. Hawthorn flowers, which look like little white roses but tend to smell bad, are often visited by bees and make good honey.

Look for: Oval leaves are wide and toothed, 1–2" long. Red-spotted white flowers in clusters. Small black fruits are tasteless. Long, straight, sharp thorns in a thick mass of branches. Thicket-forming.

Shape and Height: Round; to 40'; often much shorter and shrublike.

Habitat: Mountains, along streams and in valleys.

Range: Southwestern Canada and parts of western U.S.

Caution: Branches are covered with sharp thorns.

DOWNY HAWTHORN
Crataegus mollis

Look for: A short tree with twisted branches forming a rounded crown. Wide triangular leaves 3–4" long, sharp-toothed. Thorns 2" long, narrow, straight. White flowers ½–1" wide in clusters. Round scarlet fruits. **Shape and Height:** Vase-shaped; to 35'. **Habitat:** Fertile soils in open woods. **Range:** Southeastern Canada and central and eastern U.S.

WESTERN SERVICEBERRY
Amelanchier alnifolia

Look for: Small tree with fragrant white blossoms; forms thickets. Dark green leaves 1–3" long, quite round, coarse-toothed. Clusters of ¼"- to ¾"-wide flowers become ¼–½", purplish, round fruits; these juicy, tasty berries are enjoyed by humans, deer, and other animals. **Shape and Height:** Oval; to 20', most often a shrub. **Habitat:** Open woods on mountain slopes. **Range:** Alaska and western half of Canada and U.S.

107

CURLLEAF MOUNTAIN MAHOGANY
Cercocarpus ledifolius

M ountain mahoganies are easiest to identify in the summer and fall, when their seeds develop long, silky plumes. These special whitish, feathery "tails" act as parachutes when the western winds blow, carrying the seeds away from the mother tree. Once seeds hit the ground, the plumes twist in the breeze and plant the seeds down into the soil. Deer and cattle eat the leaves and twigs of mountain mahoganies.

LOOK FOR: Typical mountain mahogany seed plumes on shrub or short tree. Spear-shaped leaves ½–1" long, glossy green above, hairy beneath, with curled-under edges.

SHAPE AND HEIGHT: Round; to 25', usually a shrub.

HABITAT: Dry mountainous areas.

RANGE: Western U.S.

FRUITS

BIRCHLEAF MOUNTAIN MAHOGANY
Cercocarpus betuloides

LOOK FOR: Small tree or shrub with distinctive seed plumes. Leaves are birchlike, 1–1½" long, hairy beneath, with rounded teeth. Greenish-yellow, tubelike flowers in small clusters. Fruits ½" long with plumes up to 4" long. **SHAPE AND HEIGHT:** Vase-shaped; to 25', often a shrub. **HABITAT:** Dry mountainous areas. **RANGE:** Oregon to Arizona.

LEAVES

LEAVES AND FRUITS

109

EASTERN REDBUD
Cercis canadensis

LEAVES

One of the neat things about brightly flowering trees is that when they are in bloom, it's easy to tell just how many there are. Once the flowers fall, they tend to blend in with the other trees around them. If you want to know how many Eastern Redbuds are in your local woods, make sure to get out early in the spring. The redbuds will be putting on a show with their unmistakable pinkish-purple flowers.

LOOK FOR: In spring, brilliant flowers emerge before leaves. Round or heart-shaped, smooth leaves, 3–5" long; turn yellow in fall. Purplish-red flowers, ½" long, cover the tree, sprouting from twigs, branches, and even the trunk. Pinkish seedpods 2–4" long. Scaly reddish-brown bark.

SHAPE AND HEIGHT: Round; to 50'.

HABITAT: Rich, moist soils in open woods.

RANGE: Southeastern Canada and eastern half of U.S.

CATCLAW
Acacia greggii

LOOK FOR: A small tree or shrub with curved, clawlike thorns ¼–½" long. Often forms thickets. Compound, feathery leaves 1–3" long, with many very small leaflets. Sweet-smelling yellow flowers in springtime in fingerlike clusters to 2½" long. Fruit in flattened, twisted, 2"- to 5"-long brown pods. **SHAPE AND HEIGHT:** Wide-spreading; to 25', often a shrub. **HABITAT:** Arid soils. **RANGE:** Southwestern U.S.

HONEY MESQUITE
Prosopis glandulosa

LOOK FOR: Feathery foliage and 1"-long, straight thorns on reddish-brown tree. Compound leaves 5–10" long, with many small leaflets. Whitish to pale yellow flowers in 2"- to 3"-long, narrow clusters. Light brown, cylindrical seedpods 4–10" long. **SHAPE AND HEIGHT:** Wide-spreading; to 50', usually much shorter. **HABITAT:** Dry soils of grasslands and arid soils along creeks. **RANGE:** Southwestern U.S.

BARK

Here is a tree with a distinctive name—actually several of them! Variously known as "Hercules Club," "Devil's Walking Stick" (for its straight, usually thorny trunk), and "Toothache Tree" (for its medicinal properties), this small tree is perhaps best known for its foliage. The leaves (the largest compound leaves of any American tree) often spread out in the crown like an umbrella. Crushed leaves smell lemony.

LOOK FOR: Compound leaves up to 36" long and 24" wide, with 7–17 toothed leaflets. Greenish-white flower clusters produce red, then brown fruits that split open to reveal black seeds. Light gray trunk with thorny knobs.

SHAPE AND HEIGHT: Oval; to 20'.

HABITAT: Moist soils near lowland rivers and streams.

RANGE: Southeastern U.S.

COMMON PRICKLY ASH
Zanthoxylum americanum

LOOK FOR: A small tree or shrub with prickly twigs and leafstalks. Compound leaves 4–10" long, with 5–11 mostly smooth-edged leaflets; leaves look like those of true ash trees. Clusters of small greenish flowers. Brown fruit capsules split to reveal black seeds. **SHAPE AND HEIGHT:** Wide-spreading; to 25', usually a shrub. **HABITAT:** Moist soils in hills and valleys. **RANGE:** Southeastern Canada and northeastern and midwestern U.S.

COMMON HOPTREE
Ptelea trifoliata

LOOK FOR: Compound leaves shiny green, 4–10" long, with 3 leaflets; turn yellow in fall. Clusters of fragrant white flowers turn into circular, flat, papery seed capsules, each with 2 seeds. Gray bark. **SHAPE AND HEIGHT:** Vase-shaped; to 25'. **HABITAT:** Eastern woods to western mountains. **RANGE:** Parts of U.S. from Southwest to east coast.

113

STAGHORN SUMAC
Rhus typhina

LEAVES

In winter, the texture and shape of this tree's branches will look like a wild stag's antlers growing in for the year (with the velvet still covering the polished horn beneath). The plush branches and twigs separate the Staghorn from the very similar Smooth Sumac. The rich red berry clusters of both of these sumacs provide winter food for Eastern Bluebirds and other songbirds, and make a very good lemony-tasting drink.

Look for: Bright green compound leaves 12–24" long, with 11–31 toothed leaflets; turn orange-red to purple in fall. Small yellow-green flowers in large dense clusters up to 12" long. Deep red berries in large pointed clusters remain on tree in winter. Velvety spreading branches. Often grows in groves.

Shape and Height: Vase-shaped; to 35'.

Habitat: Well-drained soils at edges of fields and roadsides.

Range: Southeastern Canada and northeastern U.S.

Shining Sumac
"Winged Sumac"
Rhus copallina

Look for: A small tree or thicket-forming shrub. Compound leaves 6–14" long have 11–23 smooth-edged leaflets with wings along midribs; turn dark red in fall. Red fruits in clusters, smaller than Staghorn Sumac's. **Shape and Height:** Vase-shaped; to 10'. **Habitat:** Many soil types in open areas and along woodland edges. **Range:** Eastern half of U.S.

Poison Sumac
Toxicodendron vernix

Look for: A small tree or shrub. Compound leaves 7–16" long, with 3"- to 4"-long, smooth-edged leaflets; turn orange to red in fall. White, waxy berries in clusters; similar to Poison Ivy berries. **Shape and Height:** Wide-spreading; to 30', usually a shrub. **Habitat:** Swampy areas. **Range:** Eastern U.S. **Caution:** Very poisonous—avoid contact with any part of the plant.

AMERICAN HOLLY
Ilex opaca

In wintertime, when the other hardwoods have lost their leaves and the eastern woodlands are mostly gray, the radiant leaves and berries of the American Holly glow in the undergrowth. For centuries, people have clipped off holly boughs to brighten their doorways and living rooms. Even when the berries and leaves are dry, they cling to the branches and provide holiday cheer.

LOOK FOR: A bright evergreen tree. Shiny evergreen leaves 2–4" long with sharp, spiky edges. Female trees have ¼"-wide, round, bright red fruits.

SHAPE AND HEIGHT: Triangular; to 50'.

HABITAT: Moist soils, such as near lowland rivers and streams.

RANGE: New England to Texas.

CAUTION: Leaves are prickly.

DAHOON
"DAHOON HOLLY"
Ilex cassine

LOOK FOR: A small evergreen tree or shrub. Oval leaves 1½–3" long, mostly toothless, shiny green above. Bright red berries similar to American Holly's. **SHAPE AND HEIGHT:** Oval; to 30'. **HABITAT:** Moist soils in lowlands. **RANGE:** Coastal southeastern U.S.

POSSUM HAW
Ilex decidua

LOOK FOR: Deciduous small tree or shrub. Coarse-toothed, oval leaves 2–3" long. Clusters of bright red berries cling to light gray twigs in winter. **SHAPE AND HEIGHT:** Round; to 25', usually a shrub. **HABITAT:** Moist soils in lowlands. **RANGE:** Southeastern U.S.

LEAVES AND FRUITS

SUGAR MAPLE
Acer saccharum

LEAVES AND FRUITS

Mild days and freezing nights are the perfect early springtime combination for getting sap running in Sugar Maples. First, taps are inserted into the tree trunk for the sap to drip through. Buckets are filled with clear sugary sap, which is later made into richly colored, golden-brown syrup and candy. In summer, Sugar Maples shade some of the most beautiful eastern wildflowers, and in autumn their brilliant foliage is the highlight of the eastern forests.

Look for: Bright green leaves 3–5" long, with 5 lobes (spaces between lobes are rounded); turn yellow to red in fall. Small yellow flowers in clusters. Light green winged fruits (known as keys or samaras); V-shaped in this species. Furrowed gray-brown bark.

Shape and Height: Oval; to 100'.

Habitat: Rich, deep soils in uplands.

Range: Eastern Canada and northeastern U.S.

RED MAPLE
Acer rubrum

Look for: Maple with red buds, flowers, seeds, and leafstalks. Leaves 3–6" long, have 3 (sometimes 5) forward-pointing lobes (angles between lobes sharp); turn yellow to red in fall. Bright red, winged fruits. Light gray bark becomes rough and plated with age. Often forms almost pure "Red Maple swamps" in northern areas. **Shape and Height:** Oval; to 80'. **Habitat:** Moist to swampy soils. **Range:** Eastern Canada and U.S.; planted in western U.S.

SILVER MAPLE
Acer saccharinum

Look for: A riverside maple with fancy leaves that are 6–7" long, pale green above and silvery beneath, with 3 long, sharp-toothed, deeply cut lobes and 2 smaller lobes; turn yellow in fall. Green winged fruits are L-shaped. **Shape and Height:** Oval to 80'. **Habitat:** Moist soils, especially next to rivers and ponds. **Range:** Eastern U.S.; planted in western U.S.

119

BIGLEAF MAPLE
Acer macrophyllum

LEAVES

The American West is known for its conifers—both in numbers and size they dominate the western landscape. There are, however, some fine western hardwoods, including several maples. The only large maple on the West Coast is the Bigleaf, and it lives up to its name. Its leaves are huge. The bigger the leaves, the better the shade, so the Bigleaf Maple is widely planted as a handsome shade tree. In the wild, the Bigleaf Maple often grows with Douglas Firs and is often lushly covered with mosses.

Look for: Leaves 16–24" long, with 8"- to 12"-long leafstalks, 5 deeply cut lobes; turn yellow to orange in fall. Light yellow flowers hang in fingerlike clusters. Yellow-brown fruit, hairy and sticky at base, wings very close together.

Shape and Height: Oval; to 100'.

Habitat: Moist soils at low elevations; widely planted along streets and in parks.

Range: Southwestern Canada to California.

Vine Maple
Acer circinatum

Look for: A smooth-stemmed maple growing as part tree, part shrub; can form thickets. Leaves 3–6" long, with 7–9 lobes; turn orange to red in fall. Leaf outline fits within a circle. Reddish fruits have widespread wings, almost in straight line.
Shape and Height: Wide-spreading; to 40'; weak stems usually make it shrublike.
Habitat: Moist soils in forest understories.
Range: Southwestern Canada to California.

Rocky Mountain Maple
Acer glabrum

Look for: Small tree or shrub. Leaves 4–7" long, with 3–5 sharp-toothed lobes; turn yellow to red in fall. Fruit wings close together, not spread wide as in Vine Maple. **Shape and Height:** Oval; to 40'. **Habitat:** Moist soils in mountains. **Range:** Western half of U.S.

121

NORWAY MAPLE
Acer platanoides

Norway Maples are very handsome trees and have been imported into North America for that reason. On first glance, a Norway Maple is easily mistaken for a Sugar Maple. The main differences are the green undersides of the Norway's leaves (whitish in Sugar Maple), its milky sap (clear in Sugar), and the widely spreading wings of its samaras, or fruits (close in Sugar).

LOOK FOR: Dark green leaves, 3–8" long, with 5–7 lobes; turn yellow in fall. Flowers small and yellow, appear before leaves in spring. Samara wings spread wide apart. Has dark gray bark.

SHAPE AND HEIGHT: Oval; to 70'.

HABITAT: Variety of soils in parks and woods.

RANGE: Widely planted across U.S.; native of Eurasia.

FLOWERS

BOX ELDER
Acer negundo

LOOK FOR: The only maple with compound leaves. Leaves 4–10" long, with 3–5 toothed leaflets that are 2–5" long; turn yellow in fall. Samara wings grow close together. Push a Box Elder's leaflets together to see the typical maple leaf shape. Songbirds and squirrels enjoy its seeds. **SHAPE AND HEIGHT:** Wide-spreading; to 75'. **HABITAT:** Variety of soils; most often in moist woods. **RANGE:** Entire U.S., most common in eastern U.S.

PLANETREE MAPLE
Acer pseudoplatanus

LOOK FOR: Leaves 3–7" long, with 5 sharp-toothed lobes; turn brown in fall. Greenish-yellow, drooping clusters of flowers appear after leaves in spring. Green-brown, L-shaped samaras. **SHAPE AND HEIGHT:** Wide-spreading; to 90'. **HABITAT:** Roadsides and parks. **RANGE:** Planted across U.S.; native of Eurasia.

123

CALIFORNIA BUCKEYE
Aesculus californica

FLOWERS

The buckeyes (including the imported Horse Chestnut) are known for their outstanding blossoms, which decorate the trees in large, showy upright clusters. The flowers of the California Buckeye, the Golden State's only native buckeye, are pink and white—other species have yellow, pink, red, or white flowers. You may notice pear-shaped fruit capsules, about two to three inches long, that hold polished brown nuts.

Look for: A small tree or big shrub. Leaves 4–8" long, with 5 fine-toothed, pointed leaflets, each 4–6" long; turn brown in fall. Pink and white flowers in large clusters May–June. Bark is smooth and grayish.

Shape and Height: Wide-spreading; to 40', often grows as a shrub.

Habitat: Arid soils along coasts and in foothills to 4,000'.

Range: Sierra Nevada and coast of California.

Caution: Nuts are poisonous—do not confuse with edible chestnuts.

HORSE CHESTNUT
Aesculus hippocastanum

Look for: Large leaves with 7–9 toothed leaflets that spread out from one point, each 4–10" long. Yellow- and red-spotted white flowers in large clusters in May. Spiny, thick-shelled fruit capsules 2–2½" long hold 1–2 smooth, shiny, rich brown nuts. **Shape and Height:** Oval; to 60'. **Habitat:** Parks and gardens. **Range:** Planted in central and eastern Canada and U.S.; native of Europe. **Caution:** Nuts are poisonous.

OHIO BUCKEYE
Aesculus glabra

Look for: Large typical buckeye leaves with 5–7 fine-toothed leaflets, each 3–6" long; turn yellow to orange in fall. Pale yellow flowers in 4"- to 6"-long clusters. Brown fruit capsules 1–2" across, spiny, containing 1–3 dark brown nuts. **Shape and Height:** Wide-spreading; to 70'. **Habitat:** Moist soils along streams and in woods. **Range:** East-central U.S. **Caution:** Poisonous; do not eat nuts or other parts of this plant.

125

AMERICAN BASSWOOD
Tilia americana

The basswoods have wonderful big, lopsided leaves and funny leaflike wings that twirl their seeds down to the ground. They are easy to identify by these field marks, but in midsummer you can actually identify this tree with your eyes closed. Just listen for the loud hum of honeybees. Basswoods produce their nectar-filled flowers long after most trees have stopped blooming for the year. Honeybees swarm to the sweet blossoms, and basswoods become the noisiest trees in the neighborhood. All basswoods are commonly called "bee trees" because of the great honey that bees produce from them.

LOOK FOR: Dark green leaves 6" long, rounded, sharp-toothed; turn yellow to brown in fall. Light yellow flowers ½" wide, in small clusters; they dangle from close up 4"-long, narrow, leaflike wings, called bracts, that are separate from the true leaf. Fruits are small, brown, and nutlike.

SHAPE AND HEIGHT: Oval; to 100'.

HABITAT: Rich, well-drained soils in lowlands.

RANGE: Eastern Canada and northeastern U.S.

WHITE BASSWOOD
Tilia heterophylla

LOOK FOR: Similar to American Basswood, with smaller leaves and more flowers per cluster. Leaves dull green above, silvery beneath, 4–5" long. Yellowish flowers in clusters of 10 to 20. Small, round, brown fruits litter the ground for several seasons. **SHAPE AND HEIGHT:** Oval; to 80'. **HABITAT:** Rich soils in woods. **RANGE:** Eastern U.S.

CAROLINA BASSWOOD
Tilia caroliniana

LOOK FOR: Leaves 3–5" long, rounded or heart-shaped, green above with rusty-colored hairs beneath, edges sharp-toothed. Flowers in clusters of 8 to 15. Rust-colored fruits. **SHAPE AND HEIGHT:** Oval; to 60'. **HABITAT:** Fertile soils in lowlands. **RANGE:** Southeastern U.S.

OSAGE ORANGE
Maclura pomifera

FRUITS

PAWPAW
Asimina triloba

LOOK FOR: Small tree or large shrub. Leaves 10–12" long, smooth-edged, widest past the middle; turn yellow in fall. Six-petaled purplish flowers 2" wide. Fruits look like a cross between a potato and a banana, to 5" long; soft yellow flesh is edible. **SHAPE AND HEIGHT:** Round; to 30'. **HABITAT:** Moist, rich soils, especially along waterways. **RANGE:** Mid-Atlantic and southeastern U.S.

COMMON PERSIMMON
Diospyros virginiana

LOOK FOR: Shiny leaves dark green above and lighter beneath, 4–6" long; turn yellow in fall. Fruits 1–3" long, turn from green to orange to blackish-purple; not ready to eat until fully ripe. Persimmon wood is extremely hard and heavy. **SHAPE AND HEIGHT:** Oval; to 60'. **HABITAT:** Light, well-drained or moist, rich soils. **RANGE:** Large areas in eastern half of U.S.

Before the invention of barbed wire, ranchers took these trees, native to Oklahoma and Texas, and planted them as living fences far and wide across the prairies and plains. The needle-sharp thorns of the Osage Orange kept livestock at a distance. There are many handsomer trees in America, but the Osage Orange is still very popular and is widely planted as rows of hedges. The dimpled fruits look like oranges but have milky juice and aren't edible.

LOOK FOR: Smooth-edged, pointed leaves 3–6" long; turn yellow in fall. Orange- or grapefruit-sized fruits are wrinkly and warty. Sharp, strong, ½–1" thorns on twigs. Yellow-orange, deeply furrowed bark.

SHAPE AND HEIGHT: Wide-spreading; to 50'.

HABITAT: Moist soils; often planted in hedges.

RANGE: Widespread; native to southwestern U.S.

129

BLUEBLOSSOM
Ceanothus thyrsiflorus

FLOWERS

In the western U.S. there are many related plants known as "wild lilacs." They are mostly shrubs with handsome blue or white springtime flowers. The Blueblossom is one of the few that grow to tree size. At the edge of Redwood forests and along the coast, these trees are a beautiful sight in blossom.

LOOK FOR: A small tree or shrub that forms thickets. Dark evergreen leaves 1–2½" long, fine-toothed, narrowly oval. Light to dark blue flowers, in showy 2"- to 3"-long clusters, April–June. Fruits small, black, and sticky. Bark is reddish-brown. Common sight along west coast highways when in bloom.

SHAPE AND HEIGHT: Round; to 20'.

HABITAT: Variety of soils in forest understories and near coasts.

RANGE: Coast Ranges in Oregon and California.

EUROPEAN BUCKTHORN
Rhamnus cathartica

LOOK FOR: Small tree or shrub. Leaves 1–2½" long, dark green above and paler beneath, with rounded teeth. Twigs have thorns; small greenish flowers. Shiny black fruits. Dark brown bark. This species grows and spreads quickly and has become a pest in some areas. **SHAPE AND HEIGHT:** Vase-shaped; to 25', though usually less than half this height. **HABITAT:** Variety of soils at woodland edges and in pastures. **RANGE:** Southeastern Canada and central and eastern U.S.; native of Europe.

CAROLINA BUCKTHORN
Rhamnus caroliniana

LOOK FOR: Small tree or shrub. Long, oval leaves 2–6" long, with fine-toothed edges; turn yellow in fall. Small, 5-pointed, yellow-green flowers. Round, red to black fruits. Bark is gray and blotchy. **SHAPE AND HEIGHT:** Round; to 20'. **HABITAT:** Fertile soils in woods. **RANGE:** Southeastern U.S.

RED MANGROVE
Rhizophora mangle

LEAVES AND FRUITS

Red Mangroves are land builders. Look at the way their arching roots spread out into the salt water where they live. These roots attract all sorts of creatures and plants that live on and among them. Before long, the older roots begin to collect sand and eventually build up so much debris that they become part of the land. Red Mangrove seeds develop into sprouts while they are still attached to the mother plant. When they are finally released, they are foot-long seedlings.

LOOK FOR: Small trees with long stiltlike roots that form dense thickets. Smooth, green, leathery evergreen leaves 3–5" long. Small brownish fruit grows green sprout up to a foot long before dropping from tree. Red Mangrove grows with other species shown here but lives farthest out from the shore.

SHAPE AND HEIGHT: Wide-spreading; usually to 20', can grow to 80' in tropics.

HABITAT: Saltwater tidal creeks and estuaries.

RANGE: Florida.

BLACK MANGROVE
Avicennia germinans

LOOK FOR: Small trees or dense thicket of shrubs just inland from Red Mangroves. Oblong evergreen leaves 2–3" long. White flowers ¼–½" wide, in small clusters. Green fruit capsules 1½" long and 1" wide. **SHAPE AND HEIGHT:** Wide-spreading; to 40'. **HABITAT:** Tidal swamps. **RANGE:** Florida and Gulf Coast.

WHITE MANGROVE
Laguncularia racemosa

LOOK FOR: Spreading small tree or shrub growing inshore from Red Mangrove and Black Mangrove shoreline trees. Leathery, oval evergreen leaves 1–3" long. Small white flowers in 2"-long spikes. Oval reddish-brown fruits ½" long. **SHAPE AND HEIGHT:** Wide-spreading; to 50'. **HABITAT:** Coastal areas. **RANGE:** Florida.

133

FLOWERING DOGWOOD
Cornus florida

FRUITS

On most trees, the leaves enclosing the flower buds (called bracts) are tiny. But the Flowering Dogwood makes its big, white, petallike bracts the most brilliant part of its flower. In fact, the actual flowers are tiny and tucked in the middle of the showy bracts. One of the great glories of spring is when the Flowering Dogwood's blossoms unfold in glowing white layers across its branches. It's a spectacular nature show.

Look for: Spreading undergrowth tree. Oval leaves 3–6" long, pointed, smooth-edged; turn red in fall. Tiny greenish-white flowers surrounded by 4 showy white bracts, notched at ends and spreading 3–4" across. Bright red football-shaped fruits ½" long, in small clusters. Has dark bark.

Shape and Height: Wide-spreading; to 40'.

Habitat: Moist, rich, well-drained soils in lowlands or on lower slopes.

Range: Eastern half of U.S.

PACIFIC DOGWOOD
Cornus nuttallii

Look for: Beautiful medium-sized tree. Wide, pointed leaves 4–6" long, smooth-edged; turn orange to red in fall. Six showy, petallike white bracts surround tiny, greenish flowers. Many red capsulelike fruits in rounded clusters. Much loved and cultivated by Westerners.
Shape and Height: Oval; to 60'. **Habitat:** Moist soils in shaded coniferous forests. **Range:** Southwestern Canada to California.

RED OSIER DOGWOOD
Cornus stolonifera

Look for: Small tree or shrub with bright red twigs. Leaves 2–4" long, smooth-edged, pointed, with sunken veins; turn red in fall. White flowers and fruits in open clusters. Common in the wild and often planted as an ornamental shrub, admired for its bright red stems. **Shape and Height:** Round; sometimes small tree up to 15', usually a shorter shrub. **Habitat:** Moist soils along streams and similar areas. **Range:** Alaska, across Canada, and in western and northern U.S.

135

PACIFIC RHODODENDRON
Rhododendron macrophyllum

FLOWERS

The California Redwood forests are some of the most impressive natural areas on earth, but they can be quite dark. In the springtime, however, they are lit up by the showy pink flowers of the Pacific Rhododendron. Rhododendrons, wherever they grow, tend to form very thick, luxurious masses of branches and leaves. Animals won't find much to eat in a rhododendron thicket, but it is a good place to hide.

LOOK FOR: Spreading shrub or, rarely, a small tree. Leathery, shiny, evergreen leaves 3–10" long, with smooth, turned-under edges. Purplish-pink flowers 1–2" wide, in large showy clusters.

SHAPE AND HEIGHT: Wide-spreading; rarely up to 25', usually a shorter shrub.

HABITAT: Moist soils in temperate rain forests and Redwood forests.

RANGE: West coast of U.S.

ROSEBAY RHODODENDRON
Rhododendron maximum

LOOK FOR: Sprawling shrub or small tree that forms thickets. Smooth-edged, leathery leaves 4–10" long, dark green above and whitish beneath. Deep pinkish-purple, 5-petaled flowers in clusters. **SHAPE AND HEIGHT:** Round; to 40', though usually a shrub. **HABITAT:** Moist soils in woods and along streams. **RANGE:** Maine south to Georgia.

TREE SPARKLEBERRY "FARKLEBERRY"
Vaccinium arboreum

LOOK FOR: Shrub or small tree with crooked branches. Oval, smooth-edged leaves 1–3" long. Small white flowers look like blueberry flowers, in clusters along twigs. Round, ¼", shiny black fruits. Has dark brown, shreddy bark. **SHAPE AND HEIGHT:** Oval; to 30'. **HABITAT:** Sandy soils in clearings and woodland understories. **RANGE:** Southeastern U.S.

PACIFIC MADRONE
Arbutus menziesii

FRUITS AND LEAVES

The Pacific Madrone, like the sycamores, has bark that is a dead giveaway. Usually, the bark is bright reddish-brown and peels off in places in large thin flakes to show its green, yellow, and gray inner bark. The rich, exciting colors of the bark make the Pacific Madrone a favorite for landscaping in the Pacific Northwest. Many birds are attracted to the madrone's orange-red, berrylike fruits.

Look for: Dark green, shiny evergreen leaves 4–6" long, smooth-edged or fine-toothed. Many small white flowers in 6"-long clusters. Bright red, round fruits ½" wide, in clusters. Richly patterned bark.

Shape and Height: Wide-spreading; to 70', often shorter and with multiple trunks.

Habitat: Variety of soils in canyons and forest understories; planted in towns.

Range: Southwestern Canada and west coast of U.S.

FLOWERS

SOURWOOD
Oxydendrum arboreum

Look for: Oval, light green, saw-toothed leaves 4–6" long; turn red in fall. White bell-like flowers look like flowers of Lily of the Valley, in 6"- to 10"-long drooping clusters in midsummer. In summer covered with flowers and buzzing bees. **Shape and Height:** Oval; to 60'. **Habitat:** Well-drained soils in valleys and on hills. **Range:** Southeastern U.S.

SOUTHERN CATALPA
Catalpa bignioides

L ike the buckeyes, catalpas are showy but messy. People who plant them next to their houses or driveways are always cleaning up after these trees. The Southern Catalpa's big, sticky leaves, huge seed capsules, and masses of brown- and purple-spotted white flowers make it easy to identify, but they look a lot better on the tree than on the family car.

LOOK FOR: Foot-long, dull green, heart-shaped leaves; turn blackish in fall. Tubular, purple-and-brown-spotted, white flowers in 6"- to 10"-long clusters. Brown fruit capsules 10–20" long, look like giant bean pods; remain on tree during winter before releasing seeds in spring.

SHAPE AND HEIGHT: Oval; to 60'.

HABITAT: Rich, moist soils at woodland edges.

RANGE: Originally only southeastern U.S, now grows in entire U.S.

LEAVES AND FRUITS

DESERT WILLOW
Chilopsis linearis

LOOK FOR: Long, very narrow, toothless leaves 3–12" long and only ¼" wide. Tubular white flowers 1–1½" long, with purple and yellow markings, in showy clusters. Slender brown seed capsules 4–12" long; release winged seeds in the fall. **SHAPE AND HEIGHT:** Round; to 30'. **HABITAT:** Sandy soils in desert washes; planted as ornamental tree. **RANGE:** Southwestern U.S.

ROYAL PAULOWNIA
Paulownia tomentosa

LOOK FOR: Medium-sized shade tree with giant leaves and beautiful blossoms. Light green, heart-shaped leaves 6–15" long. Light purple, fragrant flowers 2" long, in 8"- to 12"-long clusters. Egg-shaped seed capsules 1–1½" long, contain about 2,000 tiny seeds each. Fastest growing tree—can grow 20' in 1 year as a sapling. **SHAPE AND HEIGHT:** Vase-shaped; to 40'. **HABITAT:** Open areas and waste sites. **RANGE:** Widely planted in U.S., mainly in Southeast.

141

WHITE ASH
Fraxinus americana

The White Ash is a beautiful, tall tree with large, spreading side branches. As long as the soil is rich, it grows almost everywhere east of the Rocky Mountains. Animals, especially birds, search out its nutritious seeds. White Ash wood is both tough and elastic, so it is used to make all sorts of athletic equipment, from baseball bats to bows and arrows to paddles.

LOOK FOR: Compound leaves 8–12" long, with 5–11 (usually 7) 3"- to 5"-long leaflets, dark green above and whitish beneath; turn yellow or purple in fall. Light brown, paddle-shaped fruits 1–2" long, hang in clusters. Blackish bark, in diamond-shaped ridges.

SHAPE AND HEIGHT: Oval; to 80'.

HABITAT: Moist, rich soils.

RANGE: Eastern Canada and U.S.

OREGON ASH
Fraxinus latifolia

LOOK FOR: Only west coast ash growing in the wild. Compound leaves 5–12" long, with 5–7 oval, wavy-edged leaflets; turn yellow to brown in fall. Light brown fruits 1½" long, in clusters. Seeds relished by Evening and Pine grosbeaks. **SHAPE AND HEIGHT:** Oval; to 75'. **HABITAT:** Moist soils in valleys and lower slopes. **RANGE:** West coast of U.S.

GREEN ASH
Fraxinus pennsylvanica

LOOK FOR: Compound leaves 8–12" long, with 7–9 sharp-toothed or untoothed 3"- to 5"-long leaflets; turn yellow in fall. Paddle-shaped, yellow-brown fruits (samaras) 1–2" long, hang in large clusters. Furrowed gray bark with reddish inner highlights. The most widespread American ash. **SHAPE AND HEIGHT:** Oval; to 80'. **HABITAT:** Rich, moist soils, especially along streams and rivers. **RANGE:** Central and eastern Canada and eastern half of U.S.; planted west of natural range.

LEAVES AND FRUITS

143

BLUEGUM EUCALYPTUS
Eucalyptus globulus

FRUITS AND LEAVES

Residents and visitors in coastal California don't have to look far to see a eucalyptus tree. They are everywhere—on hillsides, along streets and highways, in neat rows or scattered about. Californians have imported about 75 species of eucalyptus trees from Australia, but Bluegum is the most common. The tall, aromatic trees are planted for windbreaks.

Look for: Tall, straight tree with very aromatic foliage. Narrow, thick, evergreen leaves are bluish when young, grow 6–12" long, and hang vertically on the tree. White flowers 2" wide, covered with numerous stamens but no petals. Top-shaped bluish fruits are 1" wide. Bark shreds in long strips.

Shape and Height: Tall, narrow oval; to 140'.

Habitat: Spreads from windbreaks and other plantings.

Range: Coastal California.

Russian Olive
Elaeagnus angustifolia

Look for: Small, tough tree common in plains states. Smooth-edged leaves 1–4" long, dark green above and silvery beneath. Twigs also silvery. Fragrant, small, yellow, 4-petaled flowers. Light yellow, olivelike fruits ⅜" long. Can take great weather extremes. **Shape and Height:** Vase-shaped; to 20'. **Habitat:** Dry, sandy or clay soils. **Range:** Widely planted in U.S. as ornament and windbreak.

Tamarisk "Salt Cedar"
Tamarix chinensis

Look for: Small non-evergreen tree, but with small, light green, overlapping leaves like those of a juniper. Small pink or white flowers in 1"- to 2"-long, finger-shaped clusters. Narrow brown fruit capsules ⅛" long, in clusters. This tree can be a pest because it uses a lot of water. **Shape and Height:** Round; to 20'. **Habitat:** Moist soils along streams. **Range:** Southwestern U.S.

How to use the reference section

Hickory tree in fall

The **Glossary** beginning on the opposite page contains terms used by botanists and naturalists. If you run across a word in this book that you don't understand, check the glossary for a definition. Also in this section is a listing of **Resources**, including books, Web sites, and organizations devoted to North American trees, as well as a table for learning how to convert measurements to metrics. Finally, there is an **Index** of all the species covered in this book.

The 50 state trees

Every state has an official state tree. All 50 state trees are listed and illustrated on the next five pages. The trees are shown in alphabetical order by state. If you live in Massachusetts, for example, go across the list, looking for states beginning with the letter M; the state tree for Massachusetts is the American Elm. Not every state has chosen a single state tree. Iowa honors all oaks, while Nevada has two state trees—the Singleleaf Pinyon and the Bristlecone Pine. We show only the Singleleaf Pinyon. The common names in this list are those used by most botanists and naturalists, although they may sometimes differ from the names used by the states.

GLOSSARY

Acorn
A kind of nut that grows on an oak tree and looks as if it is wearing a cap or hat.

Amber
Tree sap that has hardened into rock over a long period of time.

Arid
Extremely dry.

Bough
A branch of a tree.

Bracts
Leaves, usually smaller than the leaves on the stem, located at the base of a flower.

Branchlet
A very small branch that usually does not have other branches growing off of it.

Broadleaf
Trees with wide, flat leaves that usually fall off in autumn. Broadleaf trees have flowers, unlike needleleaf trees.

Bud scales
Tiny leaves that look like scales and cover a plant bud before it opens.

Camouflage
Colors or patterns that help plants and animals blend in with their environments.

Catkin
A cluster of flowers shaped like the tail of a cat.

Compound
Having each leaf divided into two or more small

Maple leaves in fall color

leaves, called leaflets, on a single leafstalk.

Cone
The tough, woody seed container that grows on pines and other conifers.

Alabama	Alaska	Arizona	Arkansas	California
LONGLEAF PINE	SITKA SPRUCE	BLUE PALOVERDE	SHORTLEAF PINE	REDWOOD

    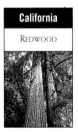

Colorado	Connecticut	Delaware	Florida	Georgia
BLUE SPRUCE	WHITE OAK	AMERICAN HOLLY	CABBAGE PALMETTO	LIVE OAK

147

GLOSSARY/THE 50 STATE TREES

Quaking Aspen page 70

Conifers
Trees that bear cones instead of fruits, such as pines and spruces.

Crown
The top of a tree. The crown gives each species its unique shape.

Cultivated
Describes plants or trees that people have developed or tended, such as flowering plants in a garden.

Deciduous
Describes trees that shed all their leaves in fall or winter.

Evergreen
Describes trees that do not lose their leaves in winter.

Fertile
Describes soil that can support a lot of plant growth.

Fertilization
The process of reproduction by which male cells combine with female cells in a flower's ovary after pollination.

Field marks
Markings, colors, shapes, and other clues to the identity of a species.

Foliage
The leaves on a plant.

Fruit
The sometimes edible growths on a flowering tree that contain the seeds.

Furrowed
Describes bark on a tree with deep grooves or lines.

Game birds
Birds that are often hunted.

Genus
A group of closely related species. Genera is the plural of genus.

Habitat
The environment in which a plant or animal lives.

Hardwoods
Broadleaf trees.

Hawaii	Idaho	Illinois	Indiana	Iowa
KUKUI	WESTERN WHITE PINE	WHITE OAK	TULIP TREE	OAKS

Kansas	Kentucky	Louisiana	Maine	Maryland
EASTERN COTTONWOOD	TULIP TREE	BALD CYPRESS	EASTERN WHITE PINE	WHITE OAK

Heartwood
The dead wood in the center of a tree trunk.

Husk
A dry shell that covers and protects seeds.

Hybrid
A plant or animal that is a mixture of two different species.

Infertile
Describes soil that cannot support much plant growth.

Keys
Winged fruits, such as those on maple and ash trees. Also called samaras.

Leafstalk
The thin stem that supports a leaf.

Lobed
Describes a leaf with deeply indented edges, such as an oak or maple leaf.

Native
A plant or animal that has originated in a particular region.

Naturalized
Describes a nonnative species that has become very common in a region, as though it were a native.

Nectar
A sweet liquid produced by flowers that attracts insects and other pollinators.

Needleleaf
Trees with needle-shaped leaves that usually do not drop off in fall. Needleleaf trees do not have flowers, unlike broadleaf trees.

Needles
Long, thin, pointy leaves, such as those on conifers.

New World
North and South America.

American Mountain Ash page 105

Massachusetts	Michigan	Minnesota	Mississippi	Missouri
AMERICAN ELM	EASTERN WHITE PINE	RED PINE	SOUTHERN MAGNOLIA	FLOWERING DOGWOOD
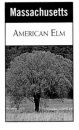	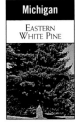		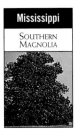	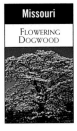

Montana	Nebraska	Nevada	New Hampshire	New Jersey
PONDEROSA PINE	EASTERN COTTONWOOD	SINGLELEAF PINYON	PAPER BIRCH	NORTHERN RED OAK
	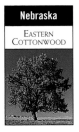			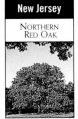

GLOSSARY/THE 50 STATE TREES

Old World
Europe and Asia.

Paired
Describes leaves that grow in twos, one on each side of the stalk.

Photosynthesis
The process by which plants use sunlight to convert water and carbon dioxide into the food that they need to grow.

Pod
A seed covering that dries out and opens when the seed matures.

Pollinate
To carry the pollen of one flower to another.

Range
The geographic area normally inhabited by a species.

Samaras
Winged fruits, such as those on maple and ash trees. Also called keys.

Sap
Liquid that flows inside a tree, carrying water and nutrients.

Sapling
A young, small tree.

Showy
Describes trees that have very large or colorful blossoms.

Shrub
A woody plant that is similar to a tree, but usually shorter and without a central trunk.

Simple
Having just one leaf on each leafstalk.

Species
A group of plants or animals that interbreeds and produces offspring. Similar species are grouped as a genus.

Stamen
The male part of a flower, made up of a filament and an anther. The stamen produces pollen.

Stand
A grove, or group of trees of the same species growing together in one area.

Temperate
A climate that is neither very cold nor very hot.

New Mexico	New York	North Carolina	North Dakota	Ohio
PINYON	SUGAR MAPLE	LONGLEAF PINE	AMERICAN ELM	OHIO BUCKEYE

Oklahoma	Oregon	Pennsylvania	Rhode Island	South Carolina
EASTERN REDBUD	DOUGLAS FIR	EASTERN HEMLOCK	RED MAPLE	CABBAGE PALMETTO

Thicket
A thick, dense area of trees and shrubs.

Toothed
Having a jagged edge, like the blade of a saw.

Treeline
The point on a mountan where it becomes too high for trees to grow. Also called the timberline.

Tundra
A treeless plain of very cold areas, like the one extending from the northern coast of Canada south to Canada's evergreen forests.

Understory
The lower areas of growth in a forest, made up of small plants and shrubs.

Unpaired
Leaves that alternate on each side of the stalk, so no two leaves are ever paired opposite each other.

Wetlands
Marshes, swamps, bogs, or any land with a lot of water in the soil.

Whorl
Three or more leaves growing from the same point on a stem.

Windbreak
Trees planted close together to block wind.

Lodgepole Pines   page 49

South Dakota	Tennessee	Texas	Utah	Vermont
BLACK HILLS SPRUCE	TULIP TREE	PECAN	BLUE SPRUCE	SUGAR MAPLE

    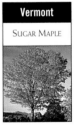

Virginia	Washington	West Virginia	Wisconsin	Wyoming
FLOWERING DOGWOOD	WESTERN HEMLOCK	SUGAR MAPLE	SUGAR MAPLE	PLAINS COTTONWOOD

 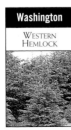 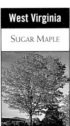 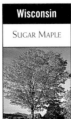 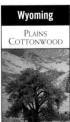

RESOURCES

Pin Oak

FOR FURTHER READING

Autumn Leaves
Ken Robbins
Scholastic Inc., 1998

The Big Tree
Bruce Hiscock
Atheneum, 1991

Discovery Box Series: Trees
Gallimard Jeunesse and Kate
Waters
Scholastic Inc., 1996

Eyewitness Books: Tree
David Burnie and Peter
Chadwick
Alfred A. Knopf, 1988

Eyewitness Handbooks: Trees
Allen J. Coombes
Dorling Kindersley, 1992

Fall Color and Woodland Harvests
C. Ritchie Bell and Anne H.
Lindsey
Laurel Hill Press, 1990

A Gift of a Tree: Book and Starter Kit
Greg Quinn
Scholastic Inc., 1994

Golden Field Guides: Trees of North America
C. Frank Brockman
Golden Books, 1986

Golden Guides: Trees
Herbert S. Zim, Alexander C.
Martin, and Dorothea Barlowe
Golden Press, 1987

Grand Trees of America: Our State and Champion Trees
Lisa Jorgenson
R. Rinehart Publishing, 1992

Look Closer: Tree Life
Theresa Greenaway
Dorling Kindersley, 1992

National Audubon Society Field Guide to North American Trees (Eastern Region/Western Region)
Elbert L. Little
Alfred A. Knopf, 1980

National Audubon Society Pocket Guide to Familiar Trees of North America (Eastern Region/Western Region)
Jerry F. Franklin and John
Farrand, Jr.
Alfred A. Knopf, 1986

The Tree Almanac: A Year-round Activity Guide
Kevin Byron and Monica Russo
Sterling Publishing, 1993

A Tree in a Forest
Jan Thornhill
Greenfield Review Press, 1991

The Tree in the Ancient Forest
Carol Reed-Jones
Dawn Publications, 1995

A Tree is Growing
Arthur Dorros
Scholastic Inc., 1997

The Tree of Time: A Story of a Special Sequoia
Kathy Baron
Yosemite Association, 1994

Trees
Jonathan Pine
HarperCollins, 1995

Trees, Leaves, and Bark
Diane Burns
NorthWord Press Inc., 1995

Why Do Leaves Change Color?
Betsy C. Maestro
HarperCollins, 1996

VIDEOS

Fall Color: Trees of the Eastern Forests
C. Ritchie Bell and Anne H.
Lindsey
Laurel Hill Press, 1992

Eyewitness: Tree
Dorling Kindersley Video, 1996

ORGANIZATIONS

American Forests
P.O. Box 2000
Washington, DC 20013
Tel: 202-955-4500
E-mail: member@amfor.org
http://www.amfor.org

Forestworld
c/o The Forest Partnership, Inc.
P.O. Box 426
Burlington, VT 05402
Tel: 802-865-1111
http://www.forestworld.com

The Holden Arboretum
9500 Sperry Road
Kirtland, OH 44094
Tel: 440-946-4400
http://www.holdenarb.org

National Audubon Society
700 Broadway
New York, NY 10003-9562
Tel: 212-979-3000 or
800-274-4201
http://www.audubon.org

The Nature Conservancy
1815 North Lynn Street
Arlington, VA 22209
Tel: 703-841-5300
http://www.tnc.org

New York Botanical Garden
200th Street and Southern Blvd.
Bronx, NY 10458
Tel: 718-817-8700

Sierra Club
85 2nd Street, 2nd Floor
San Francisco, CA 94105-3441
Tel: 415-977-5500
E-mail: information@sierraclub.org
http://www.sierraclub.org

Trees for the Future
P.O. Box 1786
Silver Spring, MD 20915
http://www.treesftf.org

Trees for the Planet
6407 32nd Street, NW
Washington, DC 20015
Tel: 202-362-TREE
E-mail: info@goodwoods.org
http://www.goodwoods.org

United States National Arboretum
3501 New York Ave., NE
Washington, DC 20002
Tel: 202-245-2726
http://www.ars-grin.gov/na

WEB SITES

Audubon's "Educate Yourself" Web site:
http://www.audubon.org/educate

International Tree Corps:
http://www.trees.org

The Missouri Botanical Garden's "What's it Like Where You Live?" Web site:
http://www.mobot.org/MBGnet

National Park Service:
http://www.nps.gov

TreePeople:
http://www.cyberjava.com/earth/tree/tree1.htm

USDA Forest Service:
http://www.fs.fed.us

World Wide Web Virtual Library—Forestry:
http://www.metla.fi/info/vlib/Forestry

Make it metric

Here is a chart you can use to change measurements of size, distance, weight, and temperature to their metric equivalents.

	multiply by
inches to millimeters	25
inches to centimeters	2.5
feet to meters	0.3
yards to meters	0.9
miles to kilometers	1.6
square miles to square kilometers	2.6
ounces to grams	28.3
pounds to kilograms	.45
Fahrenheit to Centigrade	subtract 32 and multiply by .55

INDEX

Page numbers in **bold type** point to a tree's page in the field guide.

Bluegum Eucalyptus   page 144

Ponderosa Pines   page 48

155

INDEX

Hoh Rain Forest, Olympic National Park, Washington

PHOTO CREDITS

Photo Researchers. **90a**: Bill Beatty. **90b** (inset): Bill Beatty. **91a**: David Liebman. **91b**: Joyce Photographics/ Photo Researchers. **92**: James H. Robinson. **93a**: Sonja Bullaty & Angelo Lomeo. **93b**: Eda Rogers. **93c** (inset): Ken Brate/Photo Researchers. **94a**: Emily Johnson. **94b** (inset): David Liebman. **95a**: Ernest H. Rogers/Sea Images. **95b**: Kerry Dressler. **96a**: Eliot Cohen. **96b** (inset): David Liebman. **97a**: Joy Spurr/Bruce Coleman, Inc. **97b**: David Liebman. **98a**: Joseph Nettis/Photo Researchers. **98b** (inset): Kerry Dressler. **99a**: David Cavagnaro. **99b**: Sonja Bullaty & Angelo Lomeo. **100a**: Bonnie Sue/Photo Researchers. **100b** (inset): Brock May/Photo Researchers. **101a**: Joy Spurr. **101b**: Paul Rezendes. **102a**: Kent & Donna Dannen. **102b** (inset): R. J. Erwin/Photo Researchers. **103a**: Joy Spurr. **103b**: David Liebman. **104a**: David Cavagnaro. **104b** (inset): Doug Sokell/Visuals Unlimited. **105a**: Priscilla Alexander Eastman. **105b**: Larry Miller/Photo Researchers. **106a**: Jeff Foott/Bruce Coleman, Inc. **106b** (inset): Joy Spurr. **107a**: Paul Rezendes. **107b**: Ronald J. Taylor. **108**: William H. Mullins/Photo Researchers. **109a**: Joy Spurr. **109b**: David Cavagnaro. **109c** (inset): Joy Spurr. **110a**: Christine M. Douglas. **110b** (inset): E. R. Degginger/Color-Pic, Inc. **111a**: Herbert Clarke. **111b**: David M. Schleser/Photo Researchers. **112a**: Walter S. Judd. **112b** (inset): Kerry Dressler. **113a**: Sonja Bullaty & Angelo Lomeo. **113b**: Sonja Bullaty & Angelo Lomeo. **114a**: Paul Rezendes. **114b** (inset): Sonja Bullaty & Angelo Lomeo. **115a**: Rick Cech. **115b**: E. R. Degginger/Color-Pic, Inc. **116**: John Bova/Photo Researchers. **117a**: Kerry Dressler. **117b**: Kerry Dressler. **117c** (inset): Dency Kane. **118a**: Tom Till. **118b** (inset): Bill Beatty. **119a**: John Serrao. **119b**: David Liebman. **120a**: C. G. Maxwell/Photo Researchers. **120b** (inset): Joy Spurr. **121a**: Wolfgang Kaehler. **121b**: Joy Spurr. **122**: E. R. Degginger/ Color-Pic, Inc. **123a**: David Cavagnaro. **123b**: Jane Burton/Bruce Coleman, Inc. **123c** (inset): Scott T. Smith. **124a**: Walt Anderson/Visuals Unlimited. **124b** (inset): Stephen P. Parker/Photo Researchers. **125a**: Jerry Pavia. **125b**: Bill Beatty. **126a**: Joanne Pavia. **126b** (inset): Joanne Pavia. **127a**: Sonja Bullaty & Angelo Lomeo. **127b**: David Cavagnaro. **128a**:

Richard Thom/Visuals Unlimited. **128b** (inset): Richard Parker/Photo Researchers. **129a**: Emily Johnson. **129b**: James H. Robinson. **130a**: Peter K. Ziminski/ Visuals Unlimited. **130b** (inset): Joy Spurr. **131a**: James G. Strauch, Jr. **131b**: Richard Thom/Visuals Unlimited. **132a**: Stephen G. Maka. **132b** (inset): Jeff Ripple. **133a**: James H. Robinson. **133b**: Kerry Dressler. **134a**: Thomas R. Fletcher. **134b** (inset): John M. Coffman. **135a**: Joy Spurr. **135b**: Rob & Ann Simpson. **136a**: Tom & Pat Leeson/Photo Researchers. **136b** (inset): Harry M. Walker. **137a**: Michael P. Gadomski/Photo Researchers. **137b**: Marc Epstein/Visuals Unlimited. **138a**: Joy Spurr. **138b** (inset): Joanne Pavia. **139a**: Joy Spurr. **139b**: Gale Koschmann Belinky/Photo Researchers. **140**: Michael P. Gadomski/Photo Researchers. **141a**: N. H. (Dan) Cheatham/Photo Researchers. **141b**: Rob & Ann Simpson. **141c** (inset): Joanne Pavia. **142**: Lincoln Nutting/ Photo Researchers. **143a**: Joy Spurr **143b**: David Liebman. **143c** (inset): E. R. Degginger/Color-Pic, Inc. **144a**: Bruce M. Herman/Photo Researchers. **144b**: (inset) David Cavagnaro. **145a**: Joy Spurr. **145b**: Walt Anderson. **146**: Wendell Metzen/Bruce Coleman, Inc. **147** (maple leaves): Kenneth Murray/ Photo Researchers. **147** (Alabama): Jim Steinberg/Photo Researchers. **147** (Alaska): Joy Spurr. **147** (Arizona): Rob & Ann Simpson. **147** (Arkansas): Tom McHugh/Photo Researchers. **147** (California): E. R. Degginger/Color-Pic, Inc. **147** (Colorado): Bill Beatty. **147** (Connecticut): Scott T. Smith. **147** (Delaware): John Bova/Photo Researchers. **147** (Florida): Kevin Adams. **147** (Georgia): Jack Dermid/ Photo Researchers. **148** (Quaking Aspen): Gregory G. Dimijian/Photo Researchers. **148** (Hawaii): Lindy Boyes/HVB-HNL. **148** (Idaho): Joy Spurr. **148** (Illinois): Scott T. Smith. **148** (Indiana): John Eastcott & Yva Momatiuk/Photo Researchers. **148** (Iowa): Scott T. Smith. **148** (Kansas): Rod Planck/Photo Researchers. **148** (Kentucky): John Eastcott & Yva Momatiuk/Photo Researchers. **148** (Louisiana): Jeff Ripple. **148** (Maine): E. R. Degginger/ Color-Pic, Inc. **148** (Maryland): Scott T. Smith. **149** (Mountain Ash): Rod Planck/Photo Researchers. **149** (Massachusetts): Adam Jones/Photo Researchers.

149 (Michigan): E. R. Degginger/Color-Pic, Inc. **149** (Minnesota): Eliot Cohen. **149** (Mississippi): James H. Robinson. **149** (Missouri): Thomas R. Fletcher. **149** (Montana): Charlie Ott/Photo Researchers. **149** (Nebraska): Rod Planck/Photo Researchers. **149** (Nevada): Joy Spurr. **149** (New Hampshire): David Cavagnaro. **149** (New Jersey): Christine M. Douglas. **150** (New Mexico): Lance Beeny. **150** (New York): Tom Till. **150** (North Carolina): Jim Steinberg/Photo Researchers. **150** (North Dakota): Adam Jones/Photo Researchers. **150** (Ohio): Bill Beatty. **150** (Oklahoma): Christine M. Douglas. **150** (Oregon): Geoff Bryant/Photo Researchers. **150** (Pennsylvania): E. R. Degginger/ Color-Pic, Inc. **150** (Rhode Island): David Ransaw. **150** (South Carolina): Kevin Adams. **151** (Lodgepole Pines): Lance Beeny. **151** (South Dakota): Chad Coppess/South Dakota Tourism Office. **151** (Tennessee): John Eastcott & Yva Momatiuk/Photo Researchers. **151** (Texas): Kevin Stillman/TxDOT. **151** (Utah): Bill Beatty. **151** (Vermont): Tom Till. **151** (Virginia): Thomas R. Fletcher. **151** (Washington): Joy Spurr. **151** (West Virginia): Tom Till. **151** (Wisconsin): Tom Till. **151** (Wyoming): Sherm Spoelstra. **152**: Eliot Cohen. **154–155** (Ponderosa Pines): Scott T. Smith. **155a**: (Bluegum Eucalyptus): Dan Suzio/Photo Researchers. **157**: Jim Steinberg/Photo Researchers.

*Photo Researchers, Inc.
60 East 56th Street
New York, NY 10022

Prepared and produced by
Chanticleer Press, Inc.

Publisher: Andrew Stewart
Founder: Paul Steiner

Chanticleer Staff:
Editor-in-Chief: Amy K. Hughes
Senior Editor: Miriam Harris
Managing Editor: George Scott
Associate Editor: Michelle Bredeson
Editorial Interns: Morisa Kessler-Zacharias, Abby Gordon
Photo Director: Zan Carter
Photo Editor: Ruth Jeyaveeran
Associate Photo Editor: Jennifer McClanaghan
Rights and Permissions Manager: Alyssa Sachar
Photo Assistants: Leslie Fink, Sara Jones, Karin Murphy
Photo Intern: Marie Buendia
Art Director: Drew Stevens
Designer: Vincent Mejia
Assistant Designer: Anthony Liptak
Director of Production: Alicia Mills
Production Manager: Philip Pfeifer

Contributors:
Writer: Brian Cassie
Contributing Editor: Marjorie Burns
Consultant: Susan Spackman, Colorado Natural Heritage Program
Photo Editor: Lois Safrani, Artemis Picture Research Group, Inc.
Tree Shape Paintings: Howard S. Friedman
Icons: Holly Kowitt

Scholastic Inc. Staff:
Editorial Director: Wendy Barish, Creative Director: David Saylor,
Managing Editor: Manuela Soares, Manufacturing Manager: Maria Aneiro

Original Series Design: Chic Simple Design